ISSUES

Credits and acknowledgments appear on page 128, which constitutes an extension of this copyright page.

Copyright © 2011 by Scholastic Inc.

All rights reserved.   Published by Scholastic Inc.   Printed in the U.S.A.

ISBN-13: 978-0-545-39400-0

ISBN-10: 0-545-39400-7

SCHOLASTIC, ENGLISH 3D, and associated logos are trademarks and/or registered trademarks of Scholastic Inc. Other company names, brand names, and product names are the property and/or trademarks of their respective owners. Scholastic does not endorse any product or business entity mentioned herein.

4 5 6 7 8 9 10   23   20 19 18 17 16 15 14 13 12

 Text pages printed on 10% PCW recycled paper.

SCHOLASTIC

TABLE OF CONTENTS

Academic Words in *Issues* Texts

Words to Go: High-utility words that you will encounter in other texts and content areas are **highlighted in yellow**.

Words to Know: Topic-related words that you can use to discuss and write about the issue are in **boldface**.

Does the media's focus on beauty have an ugly side?

Debate

Are video games a brain drain—or a great way to train your brain?

Data File

Since video games started coming into homes in the 1980s, their complexity and popularity keep reaching new levels.

Powering Up

Teens play video games on consoles, computers, handheld devices, and cell phones.

- According to a recent survey, 97% of teens aged 12–17 play video games.
- By gender, 99% of boys and 94% of girls enjoy this form of **entertainment**.
- 65% of game-playing teens play **socially** with other people who are in the same room. 24% of teens only play video games alone.

(Pew Research Center, 2008)

Mature Enough?

Video game ratings include E = Everyone, T = Teen, and M = Mature. The games teens list as their favorites average just above a T rating. M-rated games are the most controversial because they contain adult language and intense **violence**.

(Pew Research Center, 2008)

Out of Control

While video games are a fun activity for most players, they take over the lives of some players.

- Research shows that about 8.5% of gamers are **addicted**.
- **Addicted** teens play video games about 24 hours per week. Some play many hours more.

(Psychological Science, 2009)

Game On or Game Over?

by Oscar Gomez

Brian Alegre thought he was in control—until a video game took over his life. "I had this big urge to play all the time," he said. That urge built up to 15–20 hours of play a day. Alegre guzzled energy drinks. He started to mix up his virtual world and RL, or "real life." Brian had to face a harsh fact. He was an **addict**.

Not all players experience the dark side of video games. Michael Chaves is a professional video gamer. He thinks gaming has made him function better in real life. "I'm always thinking because, in the game, you are trying to accomplish certain tasks. If I can do it in a game, I feel I can do it in person, too."

Opinions about video games are intense. On one side, people think the games are great **entertainment**. They say, "Game on." On the other side, people think video games are **violent** and **addictive**. They say, "Game over."

According to the Pew Research Center, 94% of teen girls play video games.

Mind Games ❶

"I don't think playing video games really affects kids that much," Parker Seagren says. Seagren, a teen from Illinois, plays war and sports games with his friends. Many teens would agree with Seagren. For them, video games are just part of life. And that life includes 24/7 technology. Parents and other adults just don't get it. After all, they grew up in another century.

However, scientists know that video games do affect teens. They have gathered **evidence** about how video games **influence** the brain. When it experiences something pleasurable, the brain releases a chemical called dopamine. As a result, the brain is hard-wired to want more of that thing. It wants to press "Play Again."

Brain studies help explain why about 8.5% of teen gamers develop an **addiction** to video games. They are more likely to skip school, receive poor grades, and have **social** problems. These facts create a powerful argument against video games.

About 8.5% of teens develop an addiction to video games. They are more likely to skip school, receive poor grades, and have social problems.

However, people in favor of video games also cite brain studies. They contain **evidence** that shows the positive **influence** of video games. For example, experiments show that action video games affect parts of the brain that control vision and **coordination**. As a result, video games can improve the **ability** to pilot an aircraft, read X-rays, and perform surgery. Supporters also argue that video games make players active problem solvers. Players have to think of better ways to advance in their games.

Winners or Losers? ❷

"Video games are ruining my life," says one high school student who is **addicted** to online games. "If I'm not playing, I'm thinking about playing. I have, like, no real friends."

Some teens spend more time with video games than with friends. Critics say that video games can **distract** young people from real life. If teens are already having problems, games allow them to escape into a fantasy world. Once that happens, it is difficult for some to land back in reality.

Supporters of video games disagree that video game players

are **anti-social** loners. They say it is an exaggerated stereotype. A survey by the Pew Internet and American Life Project backs up their argument. The survey shows that gaming is often a **beneficial social** experience for teens. More than half of teens play **interactive** games with other people who are in the same room. The players work as a team. They solve problems as a group. In fact, the games **benefit** players' **social** skills rather than harm them.

Many teens play games that have positive effects. However, other teens are sucked into the world of action and first-person shooter games. It can be a world where video **violence** rules.

More than half of teens play interactive video games with other people who are in the same room. The players work as a team. They solve problems as a group.

Your Brain on Video Games

Experienced gamers mostly use the **frontal lobe**, which controls planning, problem solving, and multi-tasking.

People who don't play video games often mostly use the **parietal lobe**, which controls visualizing and spatial understanding.

Inside the brain, the **Ventral Tegmental Area** releases dopamine, a chemical that can make gaming addictive.

The **occipital lobe** controls vision. Some studies show that video games can improve players' vision.

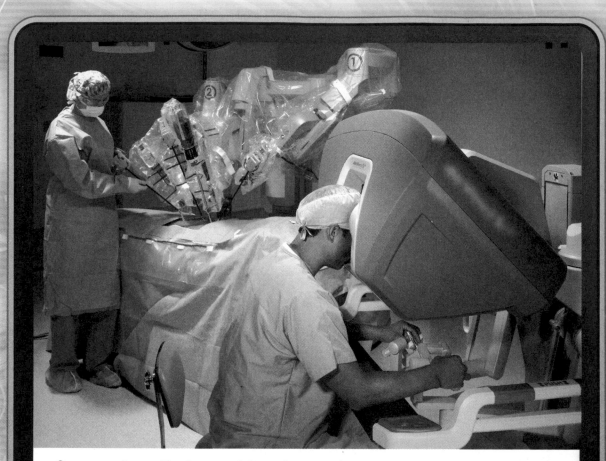

Surgeons must connect hand movements to remote movements viewed on a screen. Video games can help train them.

Combat Zone ❸

Video game **violence** is a hot-button **issue**. Some games contain extreme **violence**. That stirs up extreme emotions. These games are rated for Mature or Adult audiences. However, many teens spend **significant** amounts of time playing them.

California passed a law in 2005 that banned the sale of **violent** video games to minors. Governor Arnold Schwarzenegger said that California had a responsibility to protect children from "the effects of games that depict ultra-**violent** actions." In 2011, the Supreme Court struck down the law. The court ruled that the law violated the First Amendment, which protects freedom of speech.

Critics of the games argue that teens transfer the **violence** they see to the real world. In fact, studies have shown that the games can be negative **influences**. Both boys and girls who play M-rated games get in fights and damage property more often than teens who don't play M-rated games.

Researchers have also tested the effects of the games on teens' brains. The findings show that **violent** games have **significant** short-term effects. They raise aggression and lower self-control. However, experts point out that a small amount of video game **violence** isn't going to turn a normal teen into a criminal.

How can you know when someone's gaming is becoming a problem? Warning signs include lying about playing, withdrawing **socially**, and neglecting schoolwork. The worst sign is confusing games with real life.

No matter where people stand on the **issue**, they all agree that video games can have incredible power over players.

Technology Content Connection

Video Games to the Rescue

Disasters usually strike with little or no warning. When they happen, emergency workers need to think clearly, act fast, and work in coordination with each other. How can disaster workers train for their dangerous jobs? Video games come to the rescue.

Video games can simulate disasters such as fires, chemical spills, explosions, and hurricanes. While playing the games, emergency workers learn to make decisions and solve problems. They plot escape routes, defuse bombs, organize rescues, and provide medical attention. The games prepare them for disasters in the real world.

Take a Stand

If you could create a video game to prepare responders for one of these disasters, which would you choose? Why?

1. earthquake
2. terrorist bomb in an airport
3. electricity blackout

Junk food at school: Is it your right— or totally wrong?

Data File

American students are facing a health crisis. Is school food part of the problem? Or is it part of the solution?

A Health Crisis

Obesity has a serious **impact** on health. It can lead to diabetes, heart disease, and other life-threatening illnesses. Recent studies show that one in three American children and teens is overweight or **obese**. This rate has tripled in the last 40 years.

(American Heart Association, 2010)

Food by the Numbers

- Over 30 million students eat school lunches every day. That adds up to 150 million trays of cafeteria food per week.
- The government has **nutritional** standards for school lunches. For example, lunch cannot contain more than 30% of **calories** from fat.

(United States Department of Agriculture Food and Nutrition Service, 2009)

Junk Food for Sale

- In 2010, vending machines were **available** in 52% of middle schools and 88% of high schools. Using vending machines can be an **expensive habit**. A student can spend up to $10 a week on vending machine food.
- About 22% of students from elementary school to high school buy food in vending machines every day. The food adds an average of 253 **calories** per day to each student's diet.

(Journal of School Health, 2010)

Food Fight

by Dora Rodriguez

How do teens feel about junk food in school? Opinions range from pro-junk food to pro-health food.

"We're teenagers. We don't want healthy food," explains Kaleb Lewis, a teen from Portland, Oregon.

"I'm a quarterback on the football team," says Kayron Evans from New York. "So I've got to stay healthy, got to get my arms strong." He takes **nutrition** seriously. He regularly eats salad with his lunch.

"Lunch for me is chips, soda, maybe a chocolate ice cream taco," says Nicole Talbott. She buys her lunch at a market near school.

Essence Crum avoids junk food. The track athlete from Tampa, Florida, says, "At practice, coach is always telling me, 'You need water, you need fruits and vegetables if you want to win the race.' That motivates me to eat right."

The war on junk food in schools started about a decade ago. That is when studies revealed the **epidemic** of **obesity** in young people. Soon, the government, schools, parents, and students took sides on the issue. The food fight still goes on. Your body is the battleground.

Some teens regularly make healthy snack choices.

NO to Junk Food in School ❶

First Lady Michelle Obama admits that she loves burgers, fries, ice cream, and cake. However, she adds, "The problem is when that fun stuff becomes the **habit**. And I think that's what's happened in our culture. Fast food has become the everyday meal."

Mrs. Obama wants to **prevent** childhood **obesity**. She believes serving **nutritious** food in schools would benefit that goal.

Snacking on junk food in school adds up to about 14 extra pounds per child per school year.

The federal government will not fund junk food as part of school lunch. However, schools can still sell candy bars, soda, potato chips, and other high-fat snack foods on lunch lines or in vending machines. Many people think that is setting a bad example. One teacher says, "The message we send by having all these deals with junk-food peddlers is that this stuff is O.K." Studies indicate that snacking on junk food in school adds up to about 14 extra pounds per child per school year.

California is a leader in the **prevention** of childhood **obesity**. It was one of the first states to ban junk food in public schools. A recent study shows that the policy has been beneficial. Within three years, the trend of overweight students decreased. Education about healthy eating also helped. "Kids have no idea what a **calorie** is," says Zenobia Barlow, a California-based educator. "But when they're told they'll have to run six laps to work off a bag of chips, it starts to change behaviors."

YES to Junk Food in School ❷

Many people are against **banning** junk food in schools. They want to make all food choices **available** to students. John Dively, Executive Director of the Illinois Principals Association, says this: "An across-the-board junk-food **ban** does not teach young people how to make healthy choices. It simply removes some of their options."

For many students, school vending machines are an **appealing** option. The most popular vending machine items include candy, chips, crackers, cookies, cakes, and soft drinks. Many students use vending machine food to tide them over between lunch and dinner.

Eddie Livesay, a student from Tampa, Florida, says, "The people who go to the vending machines are the ones that have sports after school or other activities. They need the extra energy to survive the day."

Food sales also have a major financial **impact** for many schools. They use the money to buy **expensive** equipment for sports teams and other clubs. At Orange County High School in Virginia, a candy cart appears in hallways three times a day. The cart nets about $400 to $500 a week from candy sales.

"It's not so much the money as the service it offers to the kids," explains the principal. "I'd like to give our kids all the opportunities I can."

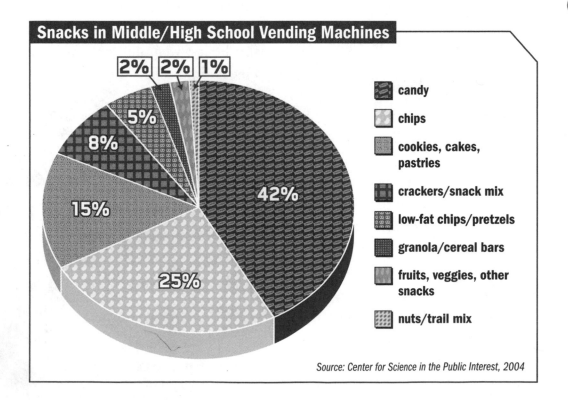

Snacks in Middle/High School Vending Machines

2% 2% 1%
5%
8%
15%
42%
25%

- candy
- chips
- cookies, cakes, pastries
- crackers/snack mix
- low-fat chips/pretzels
- granola/cereal bars
- fruits, veggies, other snacks
- nuts/trail mix

Source: Center for Science in the Public Interest, 2004

Fresh fruit is available in this middle school cafeteria line.

Who Decides? ❸

Should you have the right to eat junk food in school? Whose decision should it be?

Richard Codey, former acting governor of New Jersey, believes it's the government's responsibility to **restrict** junk food at school. "It has always been the role of government to help solve problems, especially health crises. **Obesity** is a health **epidemic** across our country."

Others argue that a child learns eating **habits** at home, not at school. "My mom's always telling me I'm going to get diabetes by the time I'm 16," says one Oregon high school freshman. He admits that he just went out for a fast food lunch with his friends.

"Being 18, technically I can be drafted into the military. But I'm not allowed to have snacks at school. That doesn't make sense."

Many students say they have the right to **select** what they eat.

Eddie Livesay puts it this way: "Being 18, technically I can be drafted into the military. But I'm not allowed to have snacks at school. That doesn't make sense."

Essence Crum doesn't think schools have to **restrict** all junk food. "If kids know what they're eating, know it's bad for them, know it's fatty food, I think they'd be more concerned about their weight." She believes teens will **select nutritious** food if they know the consequences.

What side of the debate are you on? Do teens need to be protected from junk food? Or can they learn to make their own healthy choices?

Health Content Connection

Reading a Nutrition Label

How can you tell if a food is healthy or junk? Nutrition labels give information about serving size, calories, and nutrients.

1 Serving Size A serving size is an amount of food people typically eat. The nutrition facts apply to a single serving. If the serving size is half a cup, but you eat a full cup, you will consume twice the calories and nutrients listed.

2 Calories Calories measure how much energy you get from food. A teen male needs about 2,600 calories per day, and a teen female needs 2,200.

3 Nutrients Nutrients include the proteins, minerals, and vitamins that you need to stay healthy. The numbers tell how many grams of each nutrient are in a serving. Try to choose foods that are low in fat, cholesterol, sodium, and sugar.

Nutrition Facts

1 Serving Size ½ cup (114g)
Servings Per Container 4

Amount Per Serving

2 Calories 90   Calories from Fat 30

	% Daily Value*
Total Fat 3g	**5%**
Saturated Fat 0g	**0%**
Cholesterol 0g	**0%**
Sodium 300g	**13%**
Total Carbohydrate 13g	**4%**
Dietary Fiber 3g	**12%**
Sugars 3g	
Protein 3g	

Vitamin A 80%	•	Vitamin C 60%
Calcium 4%	•	Iron 4%

*Percent Daily Values are based on a 2,000 calorie diet. Your daily values may be higher or lower depending on your caloric needs.

Take a Stand

Should all restaurants be required to provide nutrition facts? Why or why not?

Should schools be responsible for punishing cyberbullies?

Data File

The new bully is an invisible enemy that can attack your reputation, damage your self-esteem, and invade your privacy.

What Is Cyberbullying?

Cyberbullying is purposely and repeatedly harming someone using computers, cell phones, or other **technology**. It may include:

- **harassing** someone by sending **threatening** emails, voicemails, or text messages.
- forwarding someone's private messages, photos, or videos to others without permission.
- stealing someone's password or screen name and pretending to be that person.
- setting up websites to mock someone.

How Serious Is the Problem?

Cyberbullying is a significant issue that **affects** many teens:

- 21% of 11- to 18-year-olds have been cyberbullied
- 20% of students admit to cyberbullying others
- 25% of young girls and 16% of young boys have been cyberbullied

According to research **data**, **victims** of cyberbullying feel depressed, sad, angry, and powerless. Students who are cyberbullied at school feel that school is not a safe or positive place. Cyberbullying often leads to school absences, low academic performance, and school violence.

(Cyberbullying Research Center, 2010)

The New Bully at School

by Lucas Chen

Why do so many teens cyberbully? How does it feel to be their **target**? Here are answers from two teens—one a bully, the other a **victim**.

17-year-old girl from Pennsylvania:

"I recently picked on an old friend of mine, for what I will not reveal because it was unusually cruel. However, she had done something to me that was equally as wrong, if not worse. I decided not to be a friend any longer and I spread her deepest secrets to everyone. I felt somewhat guilty…at the same time, it was a payback."

14-year-old girl from New Jersey:

"Being bullied over the Internet is the worst. It's torment and it hurts. They say, 'sticks and stones may break my bones, but words will never hurt me.' That quote is a lie, and I don't believe in it. Sticks and stones may cause nasty cuts and scars, but those cuts and scars will heal. Insulting words hurt and sometimes take forever to heal."

Cyberbullying has become a significant part of teen social life. At the same time, it has invaded school life. Most cyberbullying is done off school property, but much of the hurt, mockery, and revenge it creates takes place at school. So where does a school's **responsibility** for cyberbullying start, and where does it stop?

Cyberbullying has a damaging impact on victims.

Responsibilities vs. Rights ❶

A new middle school student in Ridgewood, New Jersey, became the **target** of cyberbullies who created a Facebook group to humiliate him. They posted ethnic slurs, mocked the boy, and gave him an insulting nickname. Other students flocked to the site and joined in the **harassment**. The boy's father came to the school's principal and begged for help.

How should the school **respond**? Many people say that the school has no **authority** to take action. The cyberbullying happened off campus and online. No physical harm was done to the boy, and no crime was committed. After all, students have a right to free speech, even if that speech is hurtful.

However, supporters of the **victim** say a student has the right to attend school without being **harassed** and humiliated. The school should guarantee its students a safe and secure place to get an education. It's not right to stand by and allow cyberbullying

to **affect** students to the point of depression or worse.

Students have a right to free speech, even if that speech is hurtful.

The Ridgewood principal's **response** balanced the school's **responsibility** with the students' rights. He alerted teachers, and they spotted the bullies taunting their **victim** at school. Then he called the bullies into his office and told them that cops were monitoring their Facebook site. The **threat** of the police worked. The site came down the next day.

We're Watching You ❷

What about cyberbullying that happens inside school? Even that is not a clear-cut issue. Many schools have an "acceptable use" policy that outlines rules for using the school's **technology**. But how do school officials find out if students are breaking the rules?

Deb Socia, a principal at a middle school in Dorchester,

Massachusetts, monitors activity and **data** on the laptops the school gives to students.

"I regularly scan every computer in the building," Socia says. "They know I'm watching. They're using the cameras on their laptops to check their hair and I send them a message and say, 'You look great! Now go back to work.'"

Does the school have a right to spy on students like this? Some parents and lawmakers think this type of monitoring falls within the school's rights, but others believe it **violates** students' privacy.

The situation gets even stickier with cell phones. A recent study **estimates** that 80% of students send text messages on their phones and 74% send picture messages.

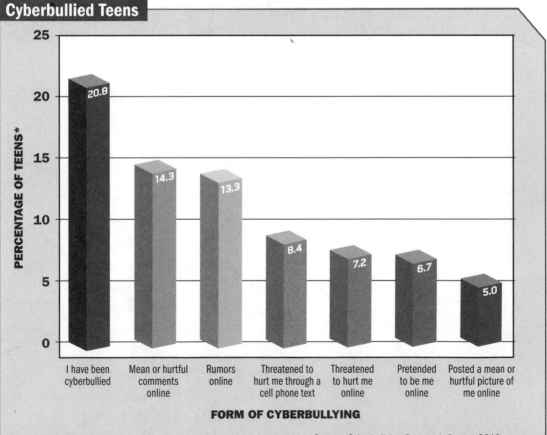

Cyberbullied Teens

PERCENTAGE OF TEENS*

- I have been cyberbullied: 20.8
- Mean or hurtful comments online: 14.3
- Rumors online: 13.3
- Threatened to hurt me through a cell phone text: 8.4
- Threatened to hurt me online: 7.2
- Pretended to be me online: 6.7
- Posted a mean or hurtful picture of me online: 5.0

FORM OF CYBERBULLYING

Source: Cyberbullying Research Center, 2010
*based on a survey of 4,441 students, ages 10 to 18

Cyberbullies can use text messages to torment their victims.

Over half use their cell phones during school hours. What if a cyberbully **threatens** a student over a cell phone while at school?

What if a cyberbully threatens a student over a cell phone while at school?

Some schools contact parents or the police but won't search the cell phones for evidence themselves. Others feel that cell phones are like backpacks. If a search is reasonably related to a school rule, like cheating, the search is legal.

Crime and Punishment ❸

What happens when a student is caught cyberbullying? Is it a crime? What is the punishment?

J.C., an eighth-grader in Beverly Hills, California, took a video of her friends making mean and sexually explicit comments about another girl and posted it on YouTube. The principal suspended J.C. for two days, and J.C.'s father sued. He said the school could not suspend his daughter "for something that happened outside of school." A judge agreed, and the school ended up paying over $100,000 in legal fees.

Many schools don't want to be "Internet police." They also don't want to get **involved** in a lawsuit. Does that mean cyberbullies can get away with anything? No, not when cyberbullying is an actual crime. Cyberbullying is criminal when it **involves threats** of violence, stalking, hate crimes, obscene text messages, or extortion.

The courts have also ruled that schools can step in to **prohibit** cyberbullying when it causes significant disruption in school or interferes with a student's right to be secure. What is a just punishment for non-criminal cyberbullying? Schools use suspensions, expulsions, and calls to parents. Some go further and notify college admission officers and potential employers.

Everyone agrees on one thing. Students should know the laws and rules about cyberbullying and be held accountable for obeying them. In general, teens are **responsible** for their own actions.

But, who is **responsible** for cyberbullying, which impacts so many—both bullies and **victims**?

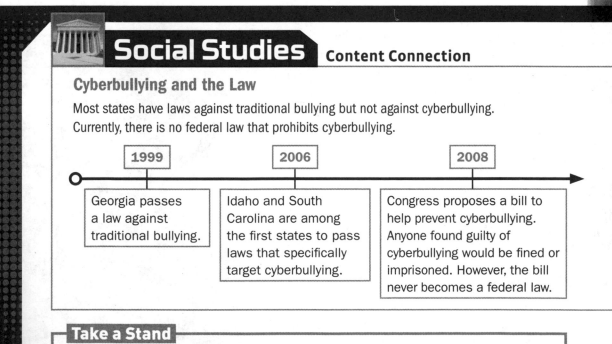

Social Studies — Content Connection

Cyberbullying and the Law

Most states have laws against traditional bullying but not against cyberbullying. Currently, there is no federal law that prohibits cyberbullying.

1999	2006	2008
Georgia passes a law against traditional bullying.	Idaho and South Carolina are among the first states to pass laws that specifically target cyberbullying.	Congress proposes a bill to help prevent cyberbullying. Anyone found guilty of cyberbullying would be fined or imprisoned. However, the bill never becomes a federal law.

Take a Stand

Should there be specific laws against cyberbullying? Why or why not?

Is graffiti VANDALISM or ART—or both?

Data File

Some people love it. Some people hate it. Graffiti creates more controversy than almost any other kind of self-expression.

Graffiti Glossary

graffiti: unauthorized words or drawings that are painted, scratched, or scribbled	throwups: quickly done bubble letters or simple two-color pieces
piece: a complex, **artistic** work that requires skill and time	tag: a signature or logo
writer: someone who does **expressive** pieces	tagger: someone who only does tags

Who Does It?

- Most graffiti taggers are males between 12 and 21 years old. Approximately 15% are female.
- About 80% of graffiti is gang or tagger graffiti.

(National Crime Prevention Council, 2011)

What Are the Costs?

Graffiti **removal** costs communities about $12 billion per year (*U.S. Department of Justice, 2004*). San Francisco alone spends more than $20 million a year (*S.F. Department of Public Works, 2011*). Graffiti **artists** risk **vandalism** charges, thousands of dollars in fines, and years in jail.

The Writing on the Wall

by Kim Nguyen

They work at night covering walls, buildings, and trains with graffiti. They call themselves **artists**. The police call them **vandals**. Who are they really?

The Manhattan graffiti **artist** Alain Maridueña uses the tag KET. He views himself as an **artist**. "Wealthy building owners think that having something on the wall hurts their property values and makes people fearful," Maridueña says. "(But) young people think that writing on the wall is a form of **expression**; it's **artistic**, and it's beautiful."

Khalid Shah is the director of Stop the Violence, a gang intervention program. He believes that graffiti is not just **vandalism**, but dangerous as well. "The cause for a lot of violence involves graffiti and either crossing it out or **removing** it," he said. For example, two young men were shot dead when **removing** graffiti from a wall in Los Angeles.

Graffiti has been part of American **culture** since the 1960s and 1970s. Taggers spray-painted their designs on New York City subway cars. The trend quickly moved to other cities and became part of the urban landscape. Over the past 50 years, graffiti has been called everything from street art to crime. The writing on the wall still generates intense opinions and **criticism**.

> "Young people think that writing on the wall is a form of expression; it's artistic, and it's beautiful."

It's a Crime ❶

Graffiti **critics** often use the "broken windows theory" to explain their views. It goes like this. One broken window in a **community** encourages **vandals** to break more windows. Soon, the whole **community** becomes a target for littering, **vandalism**, and crime.

Richard Condon organized a major graffiti conference in Washington, D.C. He thinks graffiti has an impact just like a broken window. "The neighborhood begins to deteriorate, and then that invites first minor crime and then major crime. We can see this in a lot of our cities where graffiti has just taken over."

According to the Los Angeles Police Department, gang graffiti affects **communities** even more. Gangs use graffiti to **represent** their power or to challenge rivals. It isn't just property that is being **defaced**. The people in a **community** can become victims as well. The LAPD website issues this warning:

Graffiti Penalties by State*

State	Maximum Jail Time	Maximum Fine	Other Penalties
California	1 year (3 years if a felony)	$1,000 ($10,000 if more than $400 in damage)	driver's license suspension for up to 2 years
Florida	1 year (5 years if more than $1,000 in damage)	$1,000 ($5,000 if more than $1,000 in damage)	mandatory community service and minimum fine of $250 for first offense
New York	1 year	$1,000	N/A
Texas	6 months	$2,000	N/A

*as of 2011

Murals in San Franciso's Mission District attract tourists.

"When a neighborhood is marked with graffiti indicating territorial dominance, the entire area and its inhabitants become targets for violence. Anyone in the street or in their home is fair game for drive-by attacks by rival gang members. . . . Consequently, innocent residents are often subjected to gang violence by the mere presence of graffiti in their neighborhood."

It's Street Art ❷

Graffiti **artists** view themselves as **rebels**, not criminals. They believe their writing is a form of **artistic expression** and free speech. They claim that it makes a neighborhood beautiful and gives the community a **cultural identity.** For decades, the Mission District in San Francisco has been an open-air gallery for graffiti **artists** like Las Mujeres Muralistas, Barry McGee (Twist), and Juana Alicia. The Mission's graffiti appeals to tourists rather than driving them away.

A young San Francisco graffiti writer who goes by the name SAVZ is proud of his **identity** as a graffiti **artist**. "How many people can say they risk their lives, their freedom, and their well-being for their art? All graffiti writers can."

Another response to **criticism** of graffiti is that it is a victimless crime. Supporters claim that graffiti is a means of **expression** for people without money and power. It's a street **culture** that benefits a **community**. Graffiti **artist** Barry McGee puts it this way: "There's a lot of talk of how damaging graffiti is . . . but there's actually no damage. It all can be **removed** or painted over with a roller." McGee compares graffiti to the commercial advertisements that cover walls and billboards all over the country. His **critique** is that graffiti is art, but billboards just sell things. He says people with money can put their messages everywhere without punishment. Meanwhile, graffiti **artists** are prevented from **expressing** themselves.

Drawing the Line ❸

In many cities, graffiti has become a **political** issue. **Politicians** are trying to draw the line between graffiti as art and graffiti as crime. In San Diego, the police are going after graffiti offenders like never before. But San Diego graffiti **artist** Josh Peterson (Kroer) protests that the punishment does not match the crime. He **interprets** his writing as art, not crime. "It's not like we're going out and robbing a store, or harming kids or selling drugs," he says. "It's putting art on gray buildings."

Graffiti has influenced fashion, music, and other forms of art.

Bill Miles from the San Diego County Sheriff's office says gang graffiti differs from **artistic** graffiti. "Now, the difference between taggers and gangsters is that some taggers go by themselves, they're 'oners.' They have no affiliation with a crew or anything like that." Miles encourages **legal** tagging.

But how can tagging not be **illegal**? Some cities like San Francisco have created mural zones where **artists** can **express** themselves without breaking the law. Most people point out that taggers respect each other's work and wouldn't **deface** someone else's piece. In San Diego, a group called Writerz Blok is trying to get **artists** to tag on "**legal** walls."

Can graffiti taggers work within the system? On one side, law enforcement officials say that they have to. On the other side, taggers hold up their spray-paint cans and make a choice.

Fine Arts Content Connection

Artist or Vandal?

Shepard Fairey moves between the halls of power in Washington, D.C., and the back alleys of Boston with equal ease. Fairey created the "Hope" poster that was the central image of Barack Obama's 2008 campaign for president.

Three weeks' after the presidential portrait was hung in the National Portrait Gallery, police arrested Fairey in Boston. They accused him of illegally posting his work on walls around the city. The police are also cracking down on other famous street artists like Banksy and Twist.

Shepard Fairey became known for his OBEY campaign of stickers, posters, and stencils featuring Andre the Giant.

Take a Stand

Is the crackdown on graffiti going too far? Would you report any of these people to the police?

1. a recognized artist like Shepard Fairey or Banksy
2. a local writer who does amazing pieces
3. a gang member tagging his territory
4. a tagger who sprays your property

Debate

SHOULD FEMALE ATHLETES BE ALLOWED TO PLAY WITH THE BOYS?

Data File

Title IX changed U.S. sports. As a result of the law, more girls are running onto the playing field—sometimes on boys' teams.

In 1972, Congress passed Title IX, which states that schools receiving government money cannot treat girls and boys differently. The law prohibits **gender discrimination** in all aspects of education, including **athletics**, academics, and testing.

Who Plays?

- In 1971, fewer than 300,000 girls **competed** in high school sports. Today, the number is more than 3 million (*National Federation of State High School Associations, 2010*).

- 1,249 high school girls played football and 859 played baseball in 2009–2010 (*National Federation of State High School Associations, 2010*).

- Although 57% of college students are women, only 43% of college **athletes** are women and they receive only 37% of **athletic** funding (*National Coalition for Women and Girls in Education, 2008*).

What's the Risk?

- High school **athletes** suffer 1.4 million injuries each year.

- High school girls who participate on basketball teams suffer concussions at more than two times the rate of boys.

(Center for Injury Research and Policy, 2008)

FACE-OFF ON THE PLAYING FIELD

by Judith B. Stamper

Jaime (jay-mee) Nared of Oregon stood more than six feet tall in sixth grade and played basketball in a private boys' league. After scoring 30 points in one game, she was told that she could no longer play on the team. She started playing with older girls instead.

In contrast, Jade Montgomery of North Carolina ran onto her school's football field without a struggle. After kicking a winning point, she was crowned Homecoming Queen in her football uniform.

Nared and Montgomery are just two of the thousands of girls who have **competed** on boys' sports teams. Each girl has her own story of support or **discrimination**, success or defeat. Forty years after Title IX changed school sports, the **debate** goes on. Should girls be allowed to compete on boys' sports teams?

TOUGH ENOUGH? ❶

"It's obvious. Girls are just different than guys," says a male high school **athlete**. **Opponents** of girls playing on boys' teams make the case that girls are smaller, weaker, and less **aggressive** than boys. They say that playing **contact sports** like football and wrestling puts girls at risk of serious physical harm. It also takes away girls' femininity and makes them the target of ridicule and scorn.

Jade Montgomery also plays girls' soccer and basketball.

Supporters of Title IX reject this traditional view of girls. The Women's Sports Foundation responds that girls aren't always smaller and weaker. In fact, there are greater physical differences among members of one **gender** than between **genders**. For example, the average 16-year-old girl is four inches shorter than the average 16-year-old boy. However, the heights of 90 percent of the girls span an eight-inch range.

Studies also show that sports make girls healthier, both physically and emotionally. On average, female **athletes** are stronger than girls who don't play sports. They are less likely to drink, smoke, or use drugs. Plus, they are more self-confident and goal-oriented.

FAIR PLAY? ❷

Congress passed Title IX to level the playing field for boys and girls. However, supporters of boys' sports are crying foul. They point out that many boys' teams, such as wrestling, have been cut because the school doesn't have a girls' team for the sport. They also claim that schools spend too much money on girls' sports teams and say the money should be spent on more important boys' **athletic** programs.

Title IX supporters disagree. They say that girls have been treated as second-class **athletes** for long enough. If boys' sports are getting less funding now, that is just making up for past **inequalities**. In fact, the playing field is still **biased** against girls. For example, boys' baseball programs often have better fields, equipment, and scholarships than girls' softball programs.

FOR MANY YOUNG FEMALE ATHLETES, THAT LEVEL OF COMPETITION CAN BE FOUND IN ONLY ONE PLACE—ON A BOYS' TEAM.

Young male **athletes** voice another **concern**. They say that having a girl on their team, or on an **opposing** team, is unfair. Some boys feel that it is wrong or ungentlemanly to be **aggressive** toward girls. As a result, they hold back and don't play their strongest game. Especially in **contact sports** like wrestling, many boys feel awkward about the kind of physical contact they have with girl **opponents**. Several all-male wrestling teams have forfeited rather than **compete** against a girl.

Supporters of female **athletes** respond that boys should get over it. If a girl is skilled enough to make a team, she is **capable** enough to play against as an equal. And what about outstanding young female **athletes**? These girls want to push themselves to the peak of **athletic** achievement. To do this, they need to **compete** against challenging **opponents**. For many young female **athletes**, that level of **competition** can be found in only one place—on a boys' team.

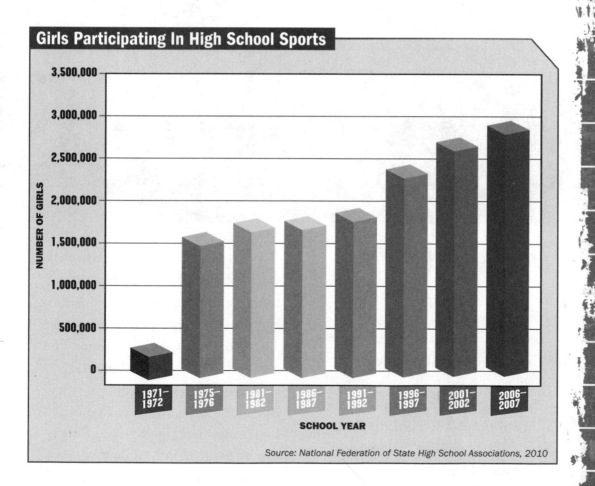

Girls Participating In High School Sports

NUMBER OF GIRLS

3,500,000
3,000,000
2,500,000
2,000,000
1,500,000
1,000,000
500,000
0

1971–1972 · 1975–1976 · 1981–1982 · 1986–1987 · 1991–1992 · 1996–1997 · 2001–2002 · 2006–2007

SCHOOL YEAR

Source: National Federation of State High School Associations, 2010

When Jaime Nared was 12, she was banned from playing on a boys' team.

GOOD SPORTS? ❸

Finally, some fans **argue** for the glory of sports. They say that sports should be about the spirit of **competition** and **athletic** excellence. Teams should not be based on quotas that force an equal number of boys and girls to play. Some people believe sports are a guy thing. Males have a love for the game that females never will.

In response to those **arguments**, supporters of girls' **athletics** point to the growing number of girls and women participating in sports. They say that Title IX changed the way girls look at sports, and the way society looks at girls. Mariah Burton Nelson, a former Stanford University basketball player, puts it this way: "Strength, independence, and freedom—those are the kind of things [girls] are learning from sports. These opportunities are changing women—and they're changing the way men and boys see women."

The **debate** is far from over. Each year, Title IX is being tested on playing fields and in courtrooms. As girls demand to play on boys' teams, boys have also begun to demand to play on girls' teams. Both on and off the playing field, boys and girls are facing off like never before.

ESPECIALLY IN CONTACT SPORTS LIKE WRESTLING, MANY BOYS FEEL AWKWARD ABOUT THE KIND OF PHYSICAL CONTACT THEY HAVE WITH GIRL OPPONENTS.

Science | Content Connection

The Biology of a Concussion

A concussion occurs from a sudden hit to the head. Spinal fluid around the brain protects it, but a hard hit can cause the brain to bang into the skull, leading to a concussion.

- High school athletes sustain more than 600,000 brain injuries every year.
- Boys' football has the highest incidence of concussions, followed by girls' soccer.
- Forty percent of high school athletes with concussions return to competition before they are ready.

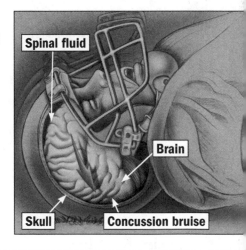

Spinal fluid

Brain

Skull

Concussion bruise

Take a Stand

Who should decide when an injured high school athlete is ready to return to the game?

1. coaches
2. doctors
3. parents/guardians

Is animal testing an experiment in cruelty?

Data File

Millions of animals die each year in laboratory experiments. Are their deaths worth it?

Animals are used in many types of research:

- scientific **experiments** on diseases, genetics, and biology
- drug testing for safety and effectiveness
- psychological research on addiction, pain, and behavior
- **toxicology** testing on pesticides, household products, and food additives
- cosmetics testing for irritation and allergies

How Many Animals?

- An estimated 30 million animals are used in biomedical research each year.
- More than 90% of animals used in research are mice, rats, and birds.

(Facts on File, 2006)

Species Specifics

Animals have made many **contributions** to medical and other research.

Cats: AIDS, eye and ear disorders	**Monkeys:** polio, cancer, heart disease
Dogs: pacemaker use, hip replacement surgery	**Rabbits:** cholesterol studies, product safety testing

(American Association for Laboratory Animal Science, 2011)

Animal Testing: Science or Shame?

by DeShawn Harris

Millions of mice and rats die each year in lab **experiments**. The animals are the best way scientists have to study and fight human diseases. But should mice die for humans to live longer and better lives?

Critics say the treatment of lab mice and rats is **cruel** and inhumane. People for the Ethical Treatment of Animals, a group known as PETA, describes animal testing like this: "The mice are slowly poisoned to death and given cancerous tumors. They are deliberately electro-shocked in pain studies and mutilated in **experimental** surgeries. They have everything from cocaine to methamphetamine pumped into their bodies."

However, supporters say the end justifies the means. John Young runs the animal testing lab at Cedars-Sinai Hospital in Los Angeles, California. Many of the rats in his lab suffer after being given brain cancer. However, the same disease will kill some of the young human patients at the hospital. "The prospect of that wipes away all doubt in my mind," Young says. "What I'm doing is not only worthwhile, but a very noble use of animals."

Rodents are the animals used most often in experiments.

Passing the Test ❶

Doctors are among the most dedicated supporters of animal testing. According to a survey by the American Medical Association, 99 percent of physicians believe that animal testing has **contributed** to the **progress** of medical **research**. Almost as many—97 percent—believe that animal testing should continue. Animal **experiments** have helped develop vaccines for polio, measles, and hepatitis. They were also key in the discovery of insulin and the study of diabetes. Animal **research** also played a **primary** part in the development of chemotherapy, heart surgery, and organ transplants. Today, **researchers** are using animals to understand and treat AIDS and Alzheimer's disease.

Animals are good **research** subjects because they are biologically **similar** to humans. They are likely to get the same

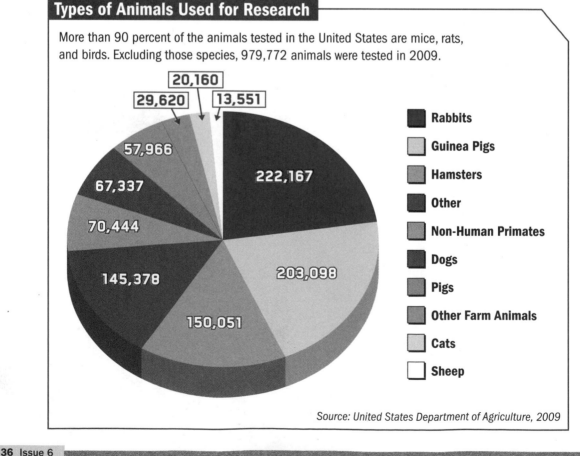

Types of Animals Used for Research

More than 90 percent of the animals tested in the United States are mice, rats, and birds. Excluding those species, 979,772 animals were tested in 2009.

20,160
29,620
13,551
57,966
67,337
70,444
222,167
145,378
150,051
203,098

- ■ Rabbits
- ▢ Guinea Pigs
- ▨ Hamsters
- ■ Other
- ▨ Non-Human Primates
- ■ Dogs
- ▨ Pigs
- ▨ Other Farm Animals
- ▢ Cats
- ▢ Sheep

Source: United States Department of Agriculture, 2009

diseases, and their reactions to disease and drugs are a good guide to how humans will react. Most importantly, they have shorter life cycles and can be studied throughout their entire lives.

Edythe London, a medical **researcher** at UCLA, points out that animals make great **contributions** to human health. "Animals allow us to test possibly life-saving treatments before they are considered safe to test on humans," she says. The animals help determine the safety of a drug and make it available for human use. This can save thousands, if not millions, of human lives.

Finally, supporters of animal testing pose an important question. Isn't it more humane to **experiment** on animals than on humans?

Failing the Test ❷

Opponents of animal testing approach the **controversy** from a different viewpoint—the animals'. They report seeing **research** animals writhing in pain, moaning, shrinking back in fear, and being killed when **experiments** are done. This happens even when rules and **regulations** are followed.

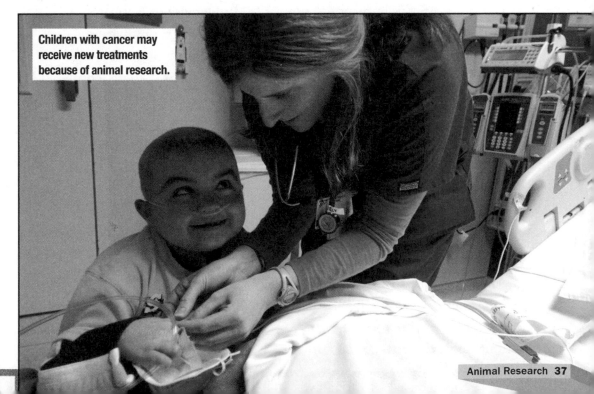

Children with cancer may receive new treatments because of animal research.

The Humane Society argues that scientists should not **rely** on animals for **cruel** tests. Their website describes the use of rabbits to test cosmetics and **toxic** products. "The test substance is put in the rabbit's eye sac, and the eyelids are held shut so the substance can get on the cornea and all around the eye. Then the eyes are rated for irritancy. This is based on redness, hemorrhaging, cloudiness, or blindness. The rabbits are held for up to 21 days and then killed."

Many critics of animal testing believe that animals have certain rights. Tom Regan is a famous thinker about animal rights. He says, "The other animals humans eat, use in science, hunt, trap, and exploit in a variety of ways, have a life of their own that is of importance to them apart from their utility to us. . . . What happens to them matters to them." Regan believes it should matter to us as well.

Is There a Middle Ground? ③

The pain and suffering caused by animal testing troubles many people. However, some of them also recognize the importance of animal **experiments** to scientific **progress**. People who support limited animal research believe that animals should suffer only when the end result is worth it. This includes saving human lives, but not testing products like cosmetics and cleansers.

People who support limited animal research believe that animals should suffer only when the end result is worth it.

In Defense of Animals is a nonprofit group that wants to **ensure** the humane use of animals in labs. "These [cosmetic] companies claim they test on animals to establish the safety of their products and ingredients for customers," says the group's website. "However, the Food and Drug Administration does not require animal testing for cosmetics. **Alternative** testing methods are widely available and lead to more reliable results."

Johns Hopkins University provides information on

alternatives to animal testing. The **alternatives** are called the 3Rs: **Replacement**, Reduction, and Refinement. In **replacement**, scientists **replace** animals and **rely** on other methods like computer models or synthetic skin to test **toxic** products. For example, many high school biology classes now practice dissection using computer programs rather than live frogs. In reduction, scientists try to use fewer animals. In refinement, **researchers** try to eliminate pain and distress for animals being tested.

Scientists, companies, and consumers are all taking a second look at the **controversy** surrounding animal testing. The number of lab animals killed in tests has fallen by almost 40 percent in recent years. Cosmetic companies have reduced their use of rabbits by about 87 percent. Some shoppers look for "**cruelty free**" labels on products. However, millions of animals still die every year in labs around the world. Are their deaths justified?

Science Content Connection

The Mouse: A Scientist's Best Friend

When scientists unlocked the genetic code of humans and mice about a decade ago, they made some amazing discoveries.

- Mice and humans have almost the same number of genes, about 30,000.

- Of all those genes, 99 percent are close matches.

Organs such as the heart and kidneys develop the same way in mice and people. However, mice have more genes that affect their sense of smell and resistance to disease. Human and mouse skeletons are very similar. Differences are mainly in the facial, hand, and foot bones. Humans even have a gene for a tail, but it is "switched off" in humans.

To study human diseases, scientists modify, or change, genes in mice. They give mice diseases like cancer, diabetes, and obesity. They create animals that do not exist in nature. These modified animals help scientists find solutions to human diseases.

Take a Stand

Should scientists change the genes of mice?

IS IT TIME TO TRASH PLASTIC BAGS?

Data File

Billions of plastic bags litter our planet. We throw them away . . . but the bags don't go away.

The Problem With Plastic

According to the Environmental Protection Agency, people in the United States use between 70 billion and 100 billion plastic bags annually. An average American family takes home 1,500 plastic bags a year, and most of those are not **recycled**. Plastic bags and products contribute to a significant **environmental** problem.

- It takes up to 1,000 years for plastic bags to biodegrade, or break down, in landfills.
- More than a million birds, marine mammals, and sea turtles die each year as a result of eating or being trapped in plastic.
- Plastic bags make up a large part of the Great Pacific Garbage Patch, a giant mass of trash **polluting** the Pacific Ocean.

(Worldwatch Institute, 2008)

Banned!

The use of plastic bags is the subject of ongoing controversy around the world. Many cities and countries have already **implemented** a ban on the **disposable** bags.

- Bangladesh banned plastic bags after they **polluted** rivers, clogged drains, and caused flooding that submerged parts of the country.
- Mexico City banned bags to cut down on the 20 million used in the city every year.
- In 2007, San Francisco became the first city in the U.S. to ban plastic bags.

(National Geographic News, 2011)

Ban It or Bag It?

by Sanjay Malik

Can you imagine a world without plastic bags? Less than 50 years ago, **disposable** plastic bags didn't exist. Now they are everywhere—in stores, homes, locker rooms, and lunchrooms. They float in the air, hang on trees, clog landfills, and **pollute** the oceans.

John Jurinek manages a San Francisco **recycling** plant. He is one of many **environmentalists** on one side of the issue. He believes the government should ban plastic bags. When asked what is wrong with the bags, he answers with one word: "Everything." To him, plastic products cause serious damage to the **environment**. Plastic bags are made from oil products and use up nonrenewable **resources**. They **litter** the air, the land, and—especially—the ocean. Plus, they never completely decompose. They just hang around forever in one toxic form or another.

On the other side of the issue are members of the plastics industry. They think the bags are just a victim of success. Today, plastic bags account for four out of every five bags handed out at a grocery store. Robert Bateman, a plastic bag manufacturer, explains that **retailers** are giving out too many bags. He argues that **consumers** are not **recycling** them properly. Concerns about the bags "need to be addressed responsibly," he says. However, he does not believe that a ban is the answer.

Plastic bags have a disastrous impact on the environment—especially marine life.

Ban the Bags ❶

Supporters of a ban note other countries, including India and China, that have successfully **implemented** bans on **disposable** bags. Many U.S. cities also want to find a way to deal with the "urban tumbleweeds" that **litter** their landscapes. San Francisco, California was the first U.S. city to pass **legislation** to ban plastic bags in 2007. Nashua Kalil works on **environmental** issues with the Zero Waste Commission in nearby Berkeley. "There is an **environmental** cost to these so-called free plastic bags," she says. "Future generations will pay that cost."

What is that cost? "The plastic bags you use will still be around long after you are," says Stephanie Barger of the Earth **Resource** Foundation, an **environmental** education group. "All the plastic that has been made is still around in smaller and smaller pieces." The bags are also much more than just an eyesore. For wildlife, they can be killers. According to Worldwatch Institute, a pro-**environment** group, tens of thousands of whales, birds, seals, and turtles die from contact with ocean-borne plastic bags. Supporters of a ban want to stop a problem that is already overwhelming.

"The plastic bags you use will still be around long after you are."

How do opponents of a ban respond? Many think that an outright ban is going too far. Judith McKenney of Silverton, Oregon says she understands the problem with plastic bags. However, she believes an individual's decision should be based on personal responsibility rather than government **legislation**. "To me, it's a matter of freedom," she adds.

Save the Bags ❷

Laurie Kusek, a spokesperson for the American Plastics Council, defends the usefulness of plastic bags for **consumers**. "It is important to understand that plastic grocery bags are some of the most **reused** items around the house," she points out. "Many, many bags are **reused** as book and lunch bags as kids head off to school, as trash can liners, and to pick up Fido's droppings off the lawn." Kusek also argues that the plastics industry is encouraging the **implementation** of **recycling** centers for the bags.

Critics of the ban argue that **consumers** will always need something to put their shopping items in. Banning plastic bags would force people to use paper bags, which create their own **environmental** problems. According to the Natural **Resources** Foundation, 14 million trees are cut down to produce 10 billion paper grocery bags each year. Also, it takes more energy to produce and **recycle** paper

A Comparison of Bags

Type of Bag	Production and Consumption	Cost to Produce	Cost to Consumer	Reusable or Disposable	Impact on Environment
Paper	Americans use over 10 billion annually, made from about 14 million trees.	5 to 8 cents per bag	free in most cities; 5 cents a bag in some areas	• disposable—15 to 20% get recycled • reusable—for wrapping/packing • biodegradable, or can be broken down	• chemicals used in production cause air/water pollution • take up about 1% of space in landfills • landfill gases lead to air pollution
Plastic	U.S. consumes 70 to 100 billion yearly, made from about 12 million barrels of oil.	1 to 2 cents per bag	free in most cities; 5 cents to $1 per bag in some areas	• disposable—less than 5% get recycled • reusable—to carry items, line trash cans, and pack • not biodegradable	• chemicals used in production cause air pollution • take up 0.4% of space in landfills • can last 1,000 years • kill many animals
Cloth/ Canvas	Five to 10% of the U.S. population uses cloth bags, which are made from polyester, cotton, or other fibers.	10 to 25 cents per bag	99 cents to $15 per bag	• reusable—for 100 or more shopping trips • not biodegradable • must be cleaned to prevent food contamination	• low impact on environment • save energy and resources

bags than plastic bags. In fact, the production of paper bags creates more air and water **pollution** than plastic bag production.

How do opponents of plastic bags respond? They point out that only one to three percent of plastic bags make it to a **recycling** center. Gordon Bennett of the Sierra Club, America's oldest **environmental** organization, offers this response on the paper versus plastic argument: "The fundamental thing about trees is that if you manage them properly they're a renewable **resource**. I haven't heard about the oil guys growing any more oil lately."

Necessary Action ❸

Ban or no ban, most people agree that something has to **occur** to stop the staggering use of **disposable** plastic bags. Erik Assadourian of the Worldwatch Institute believes that an outright ban can work in countries like India or China, but it may not be **relevant** in the U.S. He argues that a ban may not align with most Americans' belief in freedom of choice.

Instead, Assadourian supports a **tax** on plastic bags, like the one used in Washington, D.C. "In 2009,

Plastic bags are cheap for retailers, and many consumers find them useful.

A ban may not align with most Americans' belief in freedom of choice.

D.C. residents were using more than 22 million plastic bags per month," he explains. "Since a 5 cent **tax** per bag was imposed January 1, 2010, District residents are now using just

3 million plastic bags per month. And that's with just a 5 cent **tax**. Imagine what a 25 cent bag **tax** would produce."

Some **retail** stores now charge customers for **reusable** bags. **Consumers** may be surprised when this **occurs**, but they accept it. However, the real solution, many people argue, is BYOB— Bring Your Own Bag. Worldwatch Institute states on its website, "the best alternative [to plastic bags] is to carry and **reuse** your own durable cloth bags." For some Americans, that will be a challenge. However, the plastic bag problem is not going away. In fact, it will only get worse.

Can your generation give up plastic bags? The future of the planet is yours to decide.

Social Studies | Content Connection

The Great Pacific Garbage Patch

The Great Pacific Garbage Patch is a floating mass of garbage in the Pacific Ocean.

Location: midway between Hawaii and California

Contents: tons of litter, such as wrappers, plastic bags, toys, pacifiers, and toothbrushes— about 90% plastic products

Size: estimated at twice the size of Texas and 90 feet deep

Formation: The Great Pacific Garbage Patch is an ocean gyre, a system of rotating ocean currents. The Pacific Gyre pulls trash from the coast of North America and Japan.

Take a Stand

Who should be responsible for cleaning up the Great Pacific Garbage Patch?

1. governments of countries that border the Pacific Ocean
2. large corporations that manufacture plastic products
3. shipping companies that dump waste into the ocean
4. non-profit organizations that advocate for the environment

Should skipping school or failing classes keep teens out of the driver's seat?

Data File

The driving test is one test that most teens look forward to taking, but some states are now slamming on the brakes for student drivers.

"No-Pass, No-Drive"

No-pass, no-drive policies deny or **suspend** a student's driver's license because of **truancy**, poor academic performance, or school **suspension** for bad behavior.

- Twenty-seven states have no-pass, no-drive legislation.
- Florida and Texas are among the states that **require** a high school diploma, its equivalent, or enrollment and regular **attendance** in school to **obtain** a driver's permit or license.
- Kentucky and Illinois are among the states where satisfactory academic progress and school **attendance** are **mandatory** for receiving a driver's license.
- In 1988, West Virginia was the first state to implement a policy.

(Education Commission of the States, 2007)

Dropout Prevention

No-pass, no-drive policies try to discourage **truancy** and dropping out of school.

- Nationwide, 7,000 high school students drop out every day.
- Approximately 1.2 million students, or 1 out of 3 teens, fail to graduate from high school.
- About 2,000 high schools, known as "dropout factories," produce more than half of the country's dropouts.

(Alliance for Excellent Education, 2010)

Rules of the Road

by Sheena Jefferson

Clynt Goins of Athens, Tennessee, was slacking off during his junior year of high school. He was often **truant**, and his grades were in trouble. One thing Clynt really cared about was the truck he drove to school and a part-time job. When the state **suspended** his license for **truancy**, Clynt got **motivated** and refocused his priorities. "No kid wants to get stuck at home," Clynt says. He went to summer school, raised his grades, and got his license back.

Trey Ducksworth of Milwaukee, Wisconsin, ditched school when he was 16. Police officers spotted him and gave him a **truancy** ticket. Trey couldn't pay the ticket, so he ignored it, and as a result, his driver's license was **suspended**. At age 22, Trey needed a car to get to work, so he decided to drive without a license. "I was constantly getting pulled over," he recalls. "They actually took me to jail a couple of times."

Clynt Goins stands in front of his truck at McMinn County High School.

Motivation or Punishment? ❶

Do no-pass, no-drive laws **motivate** students to stay in school and graduate? Or are they a punishment that can ruin lives?

Kathy Christie of the Education Commission of the States explains why driver's licenses became a solution to **truancy** and dropping out. "[People were] looking at teenagers and asking, 'What makes them tick? What would **motivate** them to keep their nose to the grindstone and show up at school?'" The answer was obvious: **obtaining** a driver's license.

Many students also believe the policies **motivate** teens and have positive **consequences**. Matt Riley **attends** Barren County High School in Kentucky. He says, "I really think it's a good law. I think students should be held **accountable** for their grades." Stephanie Hiser, another student at the high school, agrees. "I think it's a good idea because it will make students try harder in school," she says.

Critics of the laws include Cara Roberts, a spokesperson for the Las Vegas Chamber of Commerce. She views the policies as punishment for students who are already struggling with hardships. "I don't think a person should be punished for being dealt a bad hand," Roberts said. "Punishing them further doesn't seem productive." Instead, she thinks dropouts should **obtain** vocational education and **tutoring**. That would produce better **consequences** than taking away their driving licenses.

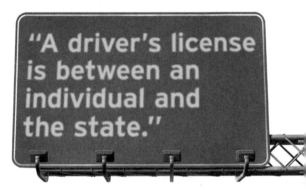

"A driver's license is between an individual and the state."

Right or Privilege? ❷

Do no-pass, no-drive laws deny students their rights as U.S. citizens? Or is driving a privilege that must be earned?

In South Carolina, lawmakers debated whether **attending** school should be a **requirement** for a driver's license. "It is a privilege to drive an automobile," Representative Bill Taylor argues. "It's not a right. All we're suggesting here is when you're 16 and 17, you need to do what you need to do as a good citizen. Stay in school."

Not everyone agrees that school **attendance** should be **mandatory** for teen drivers. The National Youth Rights Association asked for public response to the no–pass, no–drive laws. One blogger contributed this opinion: "How can they do this legally? A driver's license is between an individual and the state.

How do school boards suddenly get authority over whether a young person can drive?"

In a teen online forum about no–pass, no–drive laws, Stephanie Fehr responds that "the freedom a car represents should be a privilege." Scarlett Neveu opposes this view, arguing that driving is something that teens **require** to become responsible. "Driving shouldn't be considered a privilege. It is a

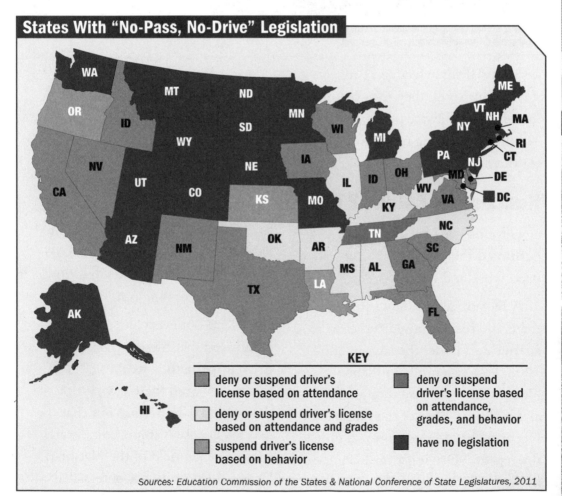

States With "No-Pass, No-Drive" Legislation

KEY

- deny or suspend driver's license based on attendance
- deny or suspend driver's license based on attendance and grades
- suspend driver's license based on behavior
- deny or suspend driver's license based on attendance, grades, and behavior
- have no legislation

Sources: Education Commission of the States & National Conference of State Legislatures, 2011

In many states, failing grades could result in a student having his or her driver's license suspended.

necessity. If some teenagers are denied this right, they miss out on learning to be aware of the safety of others and being responsible for them."

Success or Failure? ❸

Have no-pass, no-drive laws **achieved** their goals? Is all the paperwork and effort worth it?

A Florida report shows that of the 8,400 teens whose licenses were **suspended** under the laws in 2007-2008, 96% re-enrolled in school. "It confirms what we thought all along," Betty Hyle of the Florida Department of Education says of the report. "Driving a car is a great incentive for teenagers."

After Georgia passed a 1997 law that **required** the license **suspension** of a **truant** teen, the state **monitored** students' progress and observed that graduation rates improved. The **approach** seemed to be a success. However, officials say the improvement cannot be credited to just the legislation since other efforts were made at the same time to prevent dropping out.

In fact, not everyone is convinced that the no-pass, no-drive **approach** is working. "The message behind these laws is not that school is important but that the driver's license is important," states Mary Duckenfield of the National Dropout Prevention Center. "But there's no correlation between those two things. If you use that to solve the dropout problem, it's not going to work." She and many others believe that **truants** and dropouts need help and positive **motivation** to **achieve** their life goals.

For teens, one thing is clear: before you drop out or drive, learn the rules of the road.

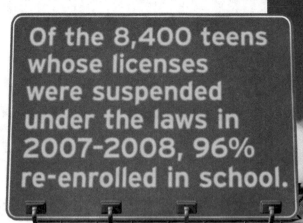

Of the 8,400 teens whose licenses were suspended under the laws in 2007-2008, 96% re-enrolled in school.

Science Content Connection

The Adolescent Brain Behind the Wheel

Reports show that car crashes are the number one killer of teens in the U.S. In 2009, eight teens age 16 to 19 died every day from motor vehicle injuries. Studies reveal three critical errors:

- driving too fast for the road conditions
- not assessing the environment around the car
- being distracted by something

Is the brain to blame? Possibly. Scientists used magnetic resonance imaging (MRI) to study normal brain development. They found that the frontal lobes, which are responsible for reasoning, judgment, and decision-making, develop last—when a person is well into his or her twenties. These late-developing frontal lobes may be responsible for teens' risk-taking while driving.

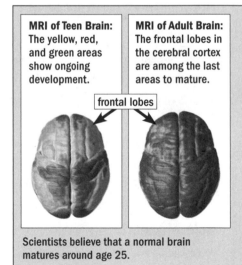

MRI of Teen Brain: The yellow, red, and green areas show ongoing development.

MRI of Adult Brain: The frontal lobes in the cerebral cortex are among the last areas to mature.

frontal lobes

Scientists believe that a normal brain matures around age 25.

Take a Stand

Should your state raise the minimum driving age? Why or why not?

Does the media's focus on beauty have an ugly side?

Data File

Perfect-looking people are everywhere—magazines, billboards, TV ads, the Internet. Do they affect how you think about your body?

Screen Time

The more **exposure** teens have to **media** such as soap operas, movies, and music videos, the more they dislike their bodies and want to be thinner.

- 54% of females who are 12 to 23 years old are unhappy with the **appearance** of their bodies *(ACOG, 2009)*.
- In movies, 58% of female characters and 24% of male characters have comments made about their looks *(Kaiser Family Foundation, 1997)*.
- Of the TV commercials aimed at teen girls, 56% used beauty as a product appeal, compared to 3% of commercials aimed at teen boys *(Kaiser Family Foundation, 1997)*.

Role Models?

- The average U.S. female model is 5'11" and weighs 117 pounds *(University of Colorado at Boulder, 2007)*.
- Most U.S. male models are 5'11" to 6'2" and weigh 140 to 165 pounds *(AskMen, 2010)*.
- If the original Barbie doll were a life-size human, she would have an **unrealistic** 36-inch chest, an 18-inch waist, and 33-inch hips *(SFGate, 2011)*.
- If a G.I. Joe action figure were a life-size human, he would have a 32-inch waist, a 44-inch chest, and 12-inch biceps *(faqs.org, 2011)*.

The Ugly Effects of Beauty

by Marcos Cano

How many **images** of beautiful people are you **exposed** to every day? Experts estimate that it can be from 1,000 to 3,000—and those **images** have a powerful influence.

"Nearly 50 **percent** of American girls in middle school and high school say they want to lose weight because of magazine pictures," says Dr. Michelle Habell-Pallan of the University of Washington.

Self-**image** issues affect both boys and girls.

"Boys are under increasing pressure to be big and muscular, just like their real-life role models," writes Michael Stetz in the *San Diego Union-Tribune*.

Do you think teens feel pressure to look like models, actors, or sports stars? Ask yourself that question the next time you look in a mirror.

Skinny Sells . . . So Do Muscles ❶

Why is the **media** filled with skinny women and muscular men? The head of Premier Model Management, a top modeling agency, explains: "Statistics have repeatedly shown that if you stick a beautiful, skinny girl on the cover of a magazine, you sell more copies. . . . At the end of the day, it is a business, and the fact is that these models sell the products."

About half of girls say they want to lose weight.

Those super-skinny models on magazine covers can also make girls see themselves as fat. But is that **realistic**? "No," says Kelly Cutrone, a fashion insider. "Models are freaks of nature. They are naturally thin and have incredibly long legs compared to the rest of their body."

"If you stick a beautiful, skinny girl on the cover of a magazine, you sell more copies."

In fact, the **media** doesn't stop with freaks of nature—they go beyond nature. A new kind of **image**-maker is ruling the fashion world—the retouch artist. These professionals alter photos of models and celebrities to make them look perfect.

When tennis star Andy Roddick **appeared** on the cover of *Men's Health* magazine in 2007, he noticed something strange about his "guns," or the biceps muscles in his arms. "I walked by the newsstand in the airport and did a total double take," Roddick says. "Little did I

know I have 22-inch guns and a disappearing birthmark on my right arm. . . . It was pretty funny."

Many people are not so amused. "The **media** impacts the way we see ourselves and who we want to be," says author Emile Zaslow. "Young people's constant pressure to be flawless, groomed, thin, and muscular can lead them to feel like their bodies are never good enough."

Dying to Be Thin ❷

Obsessing about your body can have dangerous consequences. In the United States, five million people suffer from eating **disorders**, and about 1,000 women die each year of anorexia nervosa. The disease strikes mostly young women who **perceive** themselves as fat and have such an intense fear of gaining weight that they starve themselves, sometimes to death.

Colleen was a teen victim of anorexia whose **perception** of herself didn't match reality. "I weighed less than 100 pounds and I thought I was enormous," she says. "I kept telling myself, 'If I could just lose five more pounds.' And then five after that. And so on."

During Colleen's freshman year of high school, she lost so much weight that her fingernails looked blue. A doctor said she was at risk for a heart attack.

Critics say that **exposure** to **media** contributes to girls' negative body **images**. There is no **diversity** in the way advertising models look. In fact, they weigh 23 **percent** less than the average woman. That is not an **ideal**, or even **realistic**, weight for most girls.

Laurie Mintz, a researcher on body **image**, says, "These **unrealistic images** of women have a detrimental impact on [girls] and how they feel about themselves." She suggests that magazines come with warnings like the ones on cigarette packs. "Warning: viewing these **images** is bad for your body esteem."

Katie Ford, the head of an influential modeling agency, disagrees. "The biggest problem in America is obesity," she says. "Both obesity and anorexia stem from numerous issues, and it would be impossible to attribute either to entertainment, be it film, TV, or magazines."

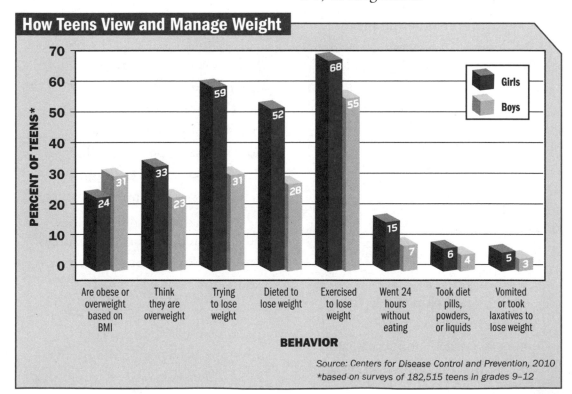

How Teens View and Manage Weight

PERCENT OF TEENS*

Behavior	Girls	Boys
Are obese or overweight based on BMI	24	31
Think they are overweight	33	23
Trying to lose weight	59	31
Dieted to lose weight	52	28
Exercised to lose weight	68	55
Went 24 hours without eating	15	7
Took diet pills, powders, or liquids	6	4
Vomited or took laxatives to lose weight	5	3

BEHAVIOR

Source: Centers for Disease Control and Prevention, 2010
*based on surveys of 182,515 teens in grades 9–12

Male models, actors, and athletes are increasingly muscular and lean.

Pumped Up ❸

Girls aren't the only ones worried about their physical **appearance**. While only 10 **percent** of anorexics are male, boys have their own issues with body **image**.

Jason Dean was skinny at age 14. The male **images** he saw in ads had buff, chiseled torsos and didn't reflect the **diverse** body types of the real world. "I saw everybody around me getting bigger," Dean says. "You see your friends getting bigger. You see athletes getting bigger."

Dean's **reaction** was to lift weights, five days a week, two hours at a time. Soon, classmates noticed that his **obsession** with

bodybuilding was not **appropriate**. "I started becoming known as that weird guy who works out all the time," he says.

However, many male teens don't stop in their quest to be bigger and stronger. A study by Oregon Health & Science University showed that 78 **percent** of high school athletes tried to improve their bodies with supplements such as creatine, ginseng, ma huang, and androstenedione. Other studies reveal that 2 **percent** of male teens use anabolic steroids, which can become a dangerous drug habit.

Can you blame this sort of unhealthy behavior on the **media**? David Zinczendo, the editor of

Men's Health magazine, says no. He defends the lean, muscular **images** that he puts on the cover of his magazine. "What's good about that **image** is that it's the picture of health," he says.

Even if **images** in the **media** don't lead to serious problems, they can still have a negative influence on teens. The Body Project, funded by the National Institutes of Health, encourages teens to **perceive** how the **media** affects them. "These people who promote the perfect body really don't care about you at all," says Kelsey Hertel, a Body Project participant. "They purposefully make you feel like less of a person so you'll buy their stuff and they'll make money."

So what advice does the Body Project give teens? "Don't try to be someone that you're not. Be yourself."

Health Content Connection

What is a Healthy Weight?

Many teens feel too thin or too fat, but few feel just right. To find out what a healthy weight is for you, figure out your body mass index, or BMI. BMI is a formula that doctors use to estimate how much body fat a person has based on his or her weight and height.

1. Calculate your BMI using an online calculator. Search "BMI calculator teens" or use the one at http://apps.nccd.cdc.gov/dnpabmi/.

2. Plot your BMI number on a chart, which tells you the percentile you are in of a group of people of the same age and gender.

3. See a health professional to interpret your BMI and get a healthy weight plan.

A healthy weight is between the 5th percentile and the 85th percentile. Someone who is in the 5th percentile has a BMI greater than 5 percent of people who are the same age and gender.

- For 13-year-old girls, a healthy BMI is 15.4 to 22.5.

- For 13-year-old boys, a healthy BMI is 15.5 to 21.8.

Take a Stand

Should schools include students' BMIs on report cards?

A Teen Anorexic Fights Back

by Ali Tate

At 16, Holly Hurt became **obsessed** with her **appearance**. The Kentucky teen couldn't wear the jeans she had worn two years before, and her boyfriend told her she needed to do crunches.

Hurt's **reaction** was to **perceive** herself as grossly overweight. She went on a starvation diet that soon spun out of control as she lost more and more weight.

"I looked like a skeleton," Hurt says. "But in my mind, if I was skinnier, I would be prettier, smarter, more popular, and just be a better person all around."

For Hurt, losing weight became an exciting challenge. The skinny models and actors she saw in the **media** were her **ideal** of perfection. She loved that she could control the amount of fat she had on her body. After a while, food—even the foods she used to love—became disgusting to her.

"When I looked in the mirror," Hurt says, "I saw that there was still more fat for me to lose."

Hurt had always been a dedicated dancer. However, after losing weight, she found dancing too challenging to continue.

> **"I was always exhausted. . . . There were times when I was carrying my books in the hallway, and I had to stop and lean against the wall."**

"I was always exhausted," she says. "I was afraid that I might pass out when I was driving. There were times when I was carrying my books in the hallway, and I had to stop and lean against the wall. I was so weak."

Finally, Hurt realized that something was wrong—terrifyingly wrong. She was starving herself, and she couldn't control it.

Hurt started seeing a doctor who specializes in eating **disorders**, and went through treatment programs. She was diagnosed as an anorexic and entered treatment at the Kentucky Center for Eating and Weight **Disorders**. She weighed only 85 pounds.

After six challenging months of treatment at the center, Hurt was able to lead a normal life. However, she couldn't forget how close she had come to starving herself to death. She wanted to educate teens about positive body **image**.

In 2009, Hurt founded the EDEN Campaign, which stands for Eating **Disorders** End Now. The campaign's website provides information about eating **disorders** and encourages people affected by them to get help. The group's slogan is "There is hope."

At college, Hurt is majoring in English, cheerleading, and leading a "completely normal 100% eating **disorder**-free life."

"Your worth is not determined by your shape or size," she says. "It's determined by who you are."

When Holly Hurt struggled with anorexia, she starved herself to lose weight.

After treatment, Hurt founded the EDEN Campaign to help others.

The Image Artist

by Pedro Gutierrez

Pascal Dangin (dahn-zhann) is the top photo retoucher in the world of fashion and **media**. His computer screen is full of people who are beautiful, but not quite perfect. Dangin's job is to make them perfect. He can look at a photograph and **perceive** exactly what it needs to catch people's eyes and make them say, "Wow, I want to look like that."

Dangin begins with real photographs of actors, models, and celebrities. Then, using sophisticated computer techniques, he improves their **appearances**. He erases wrinkles and builds up biceps; he makes eyes wider, lips fuller, and legs longer and thinner. "I look at life as retouching," Dangin says.

Dangin uses retouching tools with the eye of an artist, and most of the people in his **images** love him.

However, actor Kate Winslet once complained that he made her look too thin. She said, "I don't look like that, and more importantly, I don't desire to look like that."

Critics say that retouching photographs is misleading and wrong. It creates **images** of perfection that no real human can attain. France and the United Kingdom have considered laws that would require labels on retouched **images**.

> **"Hey, everybody wants to look good. Basically, we're selling a product— we're selling an image."**

Dangin brushes off the criticism. "Hey, everybody wants to look good," he says. "Basically, we're selling a product—we're selling an **image**. To those who say too much retouching, I say you are bogus. This is the world that we're living in. Everything is glorified."

Dangin thinks it is important for people to realize that most fashion and advertising photos are retouched. "This world is not reality," he says.

Dangin himself looks anything but **ideal**. In fact he is slightly overweight, and he dresses in comfortable, not fashionable, clothes.

"Would I want to look like that?" Dangin says of his photos. "Yes. Am I ever going to achieve that? No. Am I happy? Yes."

As a top retouching artist, Pascal Dangin changes images that appear in ads and magazines.

Does a lower minimum wage for teens pay off?

Data File

Many teens will tell you that finding a job is tough work. Is a lower minimum wage for teens the answer?

What Is the Minimum Wage?

The **minimum** wage is the lowest amount that **employers** must pay for each hour of work. The federal **minimum** wage was raised to $7.25 per hour in July 2009. Many states have their own **minimum** wages that are higher.

- A **minimum** wage **employee** who works 40 hours per week **earns** an **income** of $15,080 a year (before taxes).

- Workers younger than 20 can be paid a **minimum** wage of $4.25 per hour for the first 90 days of their **employment** (as a training period).

(United States Department of Labor, 2011)

Teen Unemployment

- The **unemployment rate** for all teens seeking jobs reached a high of 28% in 2010. Additionally, the **rate** for African Americans between ages 16 and 19 was 52%.

- In the United States, 4.2 million teens who are looking for work cannot find a job.

- Georgia has the highest **rate** of teen **unemployment** at 37%. California is second with a **rate** of 34%.

(United States Bureau of Labor Statistics, 2010, 2011)

Help (Not) Wanted

by Chris Alvarez and Julia Martinez

Adalberto Gonzalez, a 17-year-old who lives in Phoenix, Arizona, tried to find a job for more than a year. He applied for work as a cashier, a supermarket bagger, and a theater ticket seller. "There are just so many teenagers trying to apply," Gonzalez says. "Everyone fights for the same job."

High school student Jane Swett of Spring Lake, New Jersey, was one of hundreds of job seekers hoping to get a summer job at a Six Flags amusement park. "I want to work," she says. "I'm looking everywhere."

Devine Ford, 19, dropped out of school as a ninth grader. He worked for a fast-food restaurant, but then was arrested for driving without a license. He has filled out 100 job applications, but hasn't got a single callback. "Hopefully, something will change," he says. "You want to work and do right, but not having a job is stressful."

Teenagers across the country want jobs—and they need help getting them. Some people argue that lowering the **minimum** wage for teens would **increase** the number of jobs available. Others say that equal work should mean equal pay—for adults and teens alike.

Teens who earn the minimum wage are paid $7.25 per hour.

Pay Teens Less ❶

"Teen workers occupy the 'last hired, first fired' rung on the job ladder," says Heidi Schierholz. She is an **economist** at the **Economic Policy Institute**. "This has certainly been true in this recession, when teens have been hurt more than any other age group."

> **"We're at risk of having a lost generation of teens who were excluded from that valuable first job experience."**

James Sherk is a labor analyst at the Heritage Foundation. He argues that the government should set a separate, lower **minimum** wage for workers aged 16 to 19. Sherk estimates that lower **earnings** of $5.15 per hour for teens would create nearly 500,000 jobs for them.

In fact, research shows that every time the **minimum** wage goes up

10 percent, teen **employment** falls about 2 to 4 percent. The 41 percent **increase** in the **minimum** wage from 2007 to 2009 and a recession left millions of teens out of work.

Many **economists** agree that a **reduced minimum** wage would create **circumstances** that would encourage business owners to hire more teens. **Economic** data shows that **unemployment** not only impacts teens now, but also in their futures. Those who do not work as teens experience lower **compensation**, or pay, and higher **unemployment rates** for as long as 10 years later.

"We're at risk of having a lost generation of teens who were excluded from that valuable first job experience," says Michael Saltsman. He is a research fellow at the **Employment** Policies Institute. He agrees that **reducing** the **minimum** wage for teens would bring more of them into the labor market.

Equal Work, Equal Pay ❷

Opponents of a lower **minimum** wage for teens argue that the policy would have negative effects on adult workers. They maintain that the lower wage would encourage **employers** to fire adult workers and replace them with teen workers. More than most teens, adults desperately need **sufficient incomes** to provide for their families.

Adults and teens are competing for the same jobs in the **economy** following a recession. Labor expert Joseph McLaughlin explains that there just aren't enough jobs to go around. Older, more experienced workers are applying for jobs at fast-food restaurants, amusement parks, and large stores, which used to **employ** teens. "In addition, many people over the age of 55 are feeling the pinch of hard times," McLaughlin says. "They are looking for the same types of work."

Labor unions are reluctant to support a lower **minimum** wage for teenagers. They fear that jobs would **shift** from adults to teens.

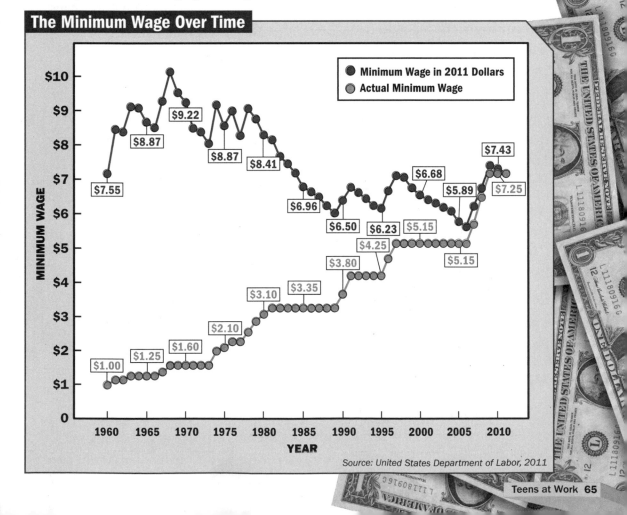

The Minimum Wage Over Time

MINIMUM WAGE

● Minimum Wage in 2011 Dollars
● Actual Minimum Wage

$9.22
$8.87
$8.87
$8.41
$7.55
$6.96
$6.50
$6.23
$5.15
$4.25
$3.80
$3.35
$3.10
$2.10
$1.60
$1.25
$1.00
$6.68
$5.89
$7.43
$7.25
$5.15

YEAR

Source: United States Department of Labor, 2011

Teens talked to possible employers at a job fair in Omaha, Nebraska.

They don't want to **increase unemployment** for older **minimum**-wage workers. They also say that two different wages for the same work could violate equal rights and amount to age discrimination. That could result in costly lawsuits against **employers**.

According to **economist** Andrew Sum of the Center for Labor Market Studies, many **employers** do not even use the lower training wage allowed for teens in their first 90 days of **employment**. They worry that it hurts morale and seems unfair.

We Want Jobs ❸

Most **economists**, politicians, and educators agree that something needs to be done. The current job market is extremely tough for teens. Carlton Tucker, a manager at a Best Buy in Washington, D.C., talked with teens at a job-training center. "We have a lot of people filling out applications who used to make $20 an hour and work in an office," says Tucker. "I try to have a mix, but it is a much harder choice to make these days to hire that teen."

Schierholz, the **economist**, believes that the best thing we can do for teen **unemployment** is nothing, at least not directly. "If we focus on turning around the **economy**, teens will be a big beneficiary of that," she says.

Economist Andrew Sum disagrees. He likes the **option** of offering **employers** a subsidy or tax credit for hiring teens. Sum also supports year-round job training programs for teens that will lead to well-paying jobs in the future.

Rick Berman, executive director of the **Employment** Policies Institute, has a different opinion. He says, "I'm a fan of job training, but I think the best job training is a job."

Teen **unemployment** does have a positive **aspect**. With fewer work opportunities, more teens are staying in school and striving for higher levels of education. Their additional degrees might mean that a **minimum**-wage job may not even be an issue in the future.

Economics Content Connection

A Monthly Minimum-Wage Budget

A minimum-wage employee who works full-time earns $15,080 a year. About $3,000 goes to taxes. The worker's take-home pay is about $12,000 a year, or $1,000 a month.

$1,000	Take-Home Monthly Income
$500	**Housing and Transportation** • Spend no more than $500 per month on rent and utilities. • Live within walking distance of work, or use public transportation or a bicycle.
$200	**Food, Toiletries, Everyday Needs** • Cook your own food and grow as much as possible. Shop at discount stores.
$30	**Cell Phone** • Stick to a basic cell phone plan.
$100	**Entertainment** • Find free activities and visit parks. Buy only basic television networks. Use free Internet at a library or other public places.
$170	**Medical Costs and Emergency Savings** • Buy basic medical insurance coverage. • Save for emergencies.

Take a Stand

Could you survive on the minimum wage?

• What part of the budget would be hardest for you?
• Is this a realistic budget for an 18-year-old?
• Is this a realistic budget for an older adult who has a child?

Scraping for College

by Marissa Menendez

Robert Partyka, a freshman at the University of Missouri, works part-time to pay for his food and social expenses. His parents pay for his tuition and room and board.

Still, he says, "We're scraping for college." The poor **economy** hurt the family because his mother lost her job and could no longer contribute to Partyka's college costs.

Partyka works at a local restaurant called Noodles and Company where he helps prepare food and take orders. He receives $7.49 an hour, 24 cents more than the federal **minimum** wage, and takes home about $200 to $250 every two weeks.

Based on his current **income**, Partyka can just meet his budget needs. Then legislators proposed a new bill in the Missouri Senate.

Senator Tom Dempsey sponsored the bill that would **reduce** the **minimum** wage for teenage **employees** to 75 percent of the state **minimum** wage. What would that mean for a teen worker like Partyka? Instead of making $7.49 an hour, he would make about $5.44 an hour.

> **On $5.44 an hour, he wouldn't be able to live on his own.**

Partyka says that the lower hourly wage would completely change his **circumstances** and his plans for the future. On $5.44 an hour, he wouldn't be able to live on his own. He would have to work more hours and take fewer college courses each semester.

The supporters of the bill in the Missouri Senate say that **reducing** the **minimum** wage for teens would **increase** job **options** for young people. However, the bill says that adults cannot be fired to hire teens at a lower wage. "I would hope that the bill would give more students jobs and opportunities," says Don Laird, Vice President of the local Chamber of Commerce. However, he adds, "I don't know if it would support that."

Opponents of the bill, like college student Karen Myers, don't think that the lower **minimum** wage would provide **sufficient** pay for many teens to make ends meet. "It's ludicrous to think it's fair to cut **earnings** for younger **employees**, some of whom—18- and 19-year-olds—are legally adults," she says. "They, too, sometimes have families to support and can barely do so with a regular **minimum** wage."

Since a coalition of young workers, labor unions, and low-**income** advocacy groups protested the bill, it hasn't come up for a vote. What does that mean for Robert Partyka and other young workers? For the time being, their paychecks—and futures—are more secure.

Working at a restaurant helps Robert Partyka earn money for food and entertainment.

Blogging With Carl Azuz

by Ganesh Khan

News anchor Carl Azuz is a familiar face to millions of middle school and high school students who watch CNN Student News in their classrooms every day. In addition to his on-screen reporting, Azuz writes about current events that are relevant to teenagers in his blog, "From A to Z with Carl Azuz."

In April 2011, Azuz tackled the issue of a lower **minimum** wage for teens on his blog. The topic of discussion was a proposed law in Maine that would create a "training wage" for teen workers. If passed, the bill would allow **employers** the **option** of paying teens $5.25 an hour rather than the state **minimum** wage of $7.50. The **reduced** wage could be paid for as long as 180 days.

Azuz explains that the argument for the training wage is that **employers** could afford to hire more workers. The argument against it is that it "devalues" young workers by paying them less than the **minimum** wage.

He asked his readers: "Would you be willing to accept $5.25/hour if your chances of getting a job were better? Or would you want to keep your current chances of getting hired—but at $7.50/hour?"

CNN Student News anchor Carl Azuz used his blog to start a discussion about a lower minimum wage for teens.

Several hundred students responded to Azuz's question, using only their first names, as required by CNN. Were they willing to accept the $5.25 training wage to have a job? Approximately 55 percent said yes, and 45 percent said no. Here are some of their responses.

Karalynn writes: "For 180 days, I think that teens can deal with a lower wage. If they are good enough for the job and can keep the responsibility of the job, then after the 180 days, they deserve the full wage/benefits of the job."

Savi writes: "We talked about this in class and we agree that this is a good idea because this opens up jobs for teens. However, it should only be from 16- to 18-years-old because after high school you need to start making a living. 180 days is way too long, but I think 90 days is just the right amount of time."

Nick writes: "What's better: a lower paying job or no job at all? Think about it, and it's only for 180 days. Most teens don't have major bills. They just want gas money and money to spend or save."

Pia writes: "People have been fighting for years to up the **minimum** wage. Just because a teenager is in training doesn't mean that they should be paid any less than an adult in training. That's simply not fair. And gas prices are still rising like crazy. Soon one hour of a teen's below-**minimum** wage pay won't even be worth a gallon of gas!"

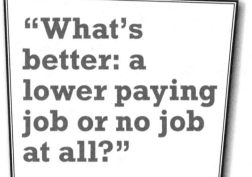

"What's better: a lower paying job or no job at all?"

Zach writes: "I am a student from Maine and the bill angers me. It tells us we are not worth as much as adult workers, and that's not true. Some families I know depend on the money that their child makes, and with this bill it could hurt the family's financial troubles."

How do you think students in your school would answer Carl Azuz's question? Would you accept a job with **compensation** less than the **minimum** wage?

Debate

Does drug testing keep schools safe— or put your rights at risk?

Data File

Across the country, students are called out of class randomly and tested for drugs. Some people believe this mandatory testing crosses the line.

Student Drug Testing and the Law

- In 1995, the U.S. Supreme Court ruled that mandatory drug testing of student athletes is legal.
- In 2002, the Court ruled drug testing of students in **extracurricular** activities constitutional.

Not a Test for Grades

In schools where mandatory drug testing occurs:

- Students are selected at **random** and excused from class to be tested for recent drug use.
- Testing is required for student athletes, drivers, and others in activities such as band.
- If a drug test is positive, the student takes follow-up tests and gets counseling. School officials notify parents or guardians but do not involve law enforcement. Test results are **confidential**.

(Source: Institute for Behavior and Health, 2011)

Percent of Drug Use Among Students

	8th Graders	10th Graders	12th Graders
Marijuana/Hashish	17.3	33.4	43.8
Inhalants	14.5	12.0	9.0
Hallucinogens	3.4	6.1	8.6
Steroids	1.1	1.6	2.0

(Source: National Institutes of Health, 2010)

Testing the Limits

by Peter V. Smith and Mia Lee Velez

In Belvidere, New Jersey, the Board of Education extended **random** drug testing in its high school to its middle school. The community had mixed reactions.

Seventh-grade student Nikko DeBenedetto thinks it is a good idea. "Kids our age shouldn't be doing drugs," he says. However, eighth grader Kenny Kane doesn't think the tests are necessary. "It's kind of an invasion of **privacy**," he says.

Noelle Komegay, a parent and teacher, believes the testing is appropriate. "It takes the pressure off [kids]. They have an easy out to say 'No. No I don't want to do this, I'm afraid I'll be tested.'" She believes testing would be beneficial for the school's **morale**.

Jay Rorty of the American **Civil Liberties** Union opposes the testing. "Making a child pee in a cup is not a good civics lesson," he argues. "It's an attempt at an easy fix to a complicated issue."

Random drug testing in schools is a complex and controversial issue. Often, students are required to submit urine, hair, or mouth swab samples. Parents must give permission. Though results are **confidential**, the **policy** tests the limits of teen illicit drug use, and it tests the limits of an **individual's** constitutional rights.

Supporters of student drug testing in school argue that it helps teens fight the pressure to use drugs.

High Stakes ❶

Random drug testing in schools puts two high stakes issues in opposition. The first is the extensive abuse of drugs in middle and high schools. The second issue is the right of **individuals** to be presumed innocent until proven guilty. The Fourth Amendment of the U.S. Constitution mandates that people are free of unreasonable search.

Drug testing in school violates American constitutional values.

Joseph A. Califano, Jr. leads the National Center on Addiction and Substance Abuse. He comments on a national survey that shows a rise in teen marijuana use. "Our nation's middle and high schools are so infested with drugs that for many students, school days have become school daze." He warns parents to "wake up to the reality that their children are going each day to schools where drug use, possession, and sale are as much a part of the curriculum as arithmetic and English."

Graham Boyd of the American **Civil Liberties** Union believes that a **policy** of **random** drug testing in school violates American constitutional values. "The presumption of innocence and the right to be free from unreasonable searches are fundamental guarantees of the Constitution," Boyd says. "**Random** student drug testing, which forces **individuals** to prove their innocence absent any suspicion of guilt, undermines these core constitutional principles."

"Prevention, Not Punishment" ❷

Advocates for student drug testing use the motto "Prevention, Not Punishment." Why? They believe testing is a **deterrent** to adolescent drug use. To support their arguments, they cite several **negative** consequences of drug abuse. According to the National Institute on Drug Abuse, drug use is responsible for poor academic performance. Also, studies reveal that drugs may be more to blame than alcohol for impaired driving.

Perhaps the most **negative** consequence is the link between early drug habits and later addiction. "The foundation for later substance use is set for most people by the time they finish high school," says Alicia C. Merline, a researcher at the University of Michigan.

Supporters of testing also argue that it **deters potential** drug use. Most teens avoid illicit drugs. In fact, a 2010 University of Michigan national survey revealed that more than 50% of high school students have never used drugs. John P. Walters is the former director of the Office of National Drug Control **Policy**. He explains that "for students who don't want to do drugs but feel pressured to try them, **random** testing gives them an iron-clad excuse for saying no."

Finally, drug-testing advocates claim the U.S. Supreme Court grants the tests' constitutionality.

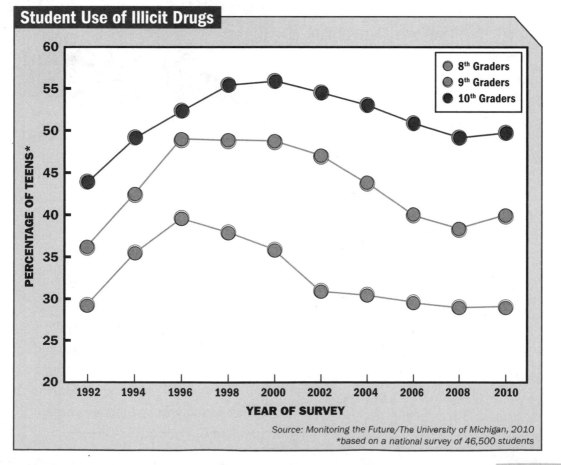

Student Use of Illicit Drugs

Legend:
- 8th Graders
- 9th Graders
- 10th Graders

PERCENTAGE OF TEENS*

YEAR OF SURVEY

Source: Monitoring the Future/The University of Michigan, 2010
*based on a national survey of 46,500 students

In the 2002 Court Decision of Pottawatomie County vs. Earls, Justice Clarence Thomas stated, "We find that testing students who participate in **extracurricular** activities is a reasonably effective means of addressing the School District's legitimate concerns in preventing, **deterring**, and detecting drug use."

"Something to Protect" ❸

Many students have refused **random** drug testing based on their beliefs. Some of those **individuals** have suffered for the decision. Allie Brody of Allentown High School in New Jersey is one of them. "I acted on my principles and stood up for fairness, **privacy**, and dignity for me and my fellow students," she says. "My school's reaction . . . was to make me an 'extracurricular exile.'"

Tony Turbeville, a math teacher in Honolulu, Hawaii, also opposes the **policy** of **random** drug testing of students and teachers. "I have nothing to hide," he asserts. "But I do have something to protect: my constitutional right to **privacy**. I am a teacher. I have a duty to teach my

Ivan Trautman, 15, of Idaho was not allowed to participate in extracurricular activities after refusing to submit to a random drug and alcohol test.

students that they have to stand up for their rights."

In addition to arguments of principle, opponents of **random** drug testing cite practical reasons. They believe that a **random** drug testing **strategy targets** students who use drugs like marijuana, which is easily detected in a urine test. This encourages the students to shift to inhalants, which are more harmful but not easily detected.

The critics also question whether this **method** of testing is truly effective, especially considering its high cost. While some tests cost less than $30 per student, others like the test for steroids can cost up to $95 per student, per test. Often, the government helps fund the programs.

Finally, **civil liberties** advocates warn that mandatory **random** drug testing could erode constitutional rights. If the trend continues, students—and in some cases, teachers—may be subject to monitoring that takes away their **private** rights as citizens.

There is one thing people on both sides of the issue agree on: drug-free schools and students.

Social Studies Content Connection

A Student's Right and a School's Wrong?

The following case came before the United States Supreme Court in 1995.

Vernonia School District Vs. Acton

James Acton, a seventh grader at Washington Grade School in Vernonia, Oregon, wanted to join the football team. His school required all student athletes to take drug tests at the beginning of the season and on a random basis during the school year. School officials had noticed a rise in student drug use in previous years.

James's parents refused to allow testing because, they said, there was no evidence that their son used drugs.

- James could not play sports for the season.
- The Acton family sued the school district.
- James's parents argued that his rights were violated under the Fourth Amendment.
- The Court ruled in favor of testing, citing that concern for the safety of student athletes overrides privacy.

> *The Fourth Amendment of the Constitution*
>
> *"The right of the people to be secure in their persons, houses, papers, and effects, against unreasonable searches and seizures, shall not be violated, and no Warrants shall issue, but upon probable cause, supported by Oath or affirmation, and particularly describing the place to be searched, and the persons or things to be seized."*

Take a Stand

If you were a judge on this case, what would you decide and why?

Presumed Guilty

by Emily C. McKenna

Loren Rasmussen, a senior at Hillsborough High School in New Jersey, spoke out against his school's **random** drug testing **policy** at the district's Board of Education meeting. He claimed he was presumed guilty, not innocent.

"Recently, I was drug tested at Hillsborough High School," Rasmussen says. "It was kind of rude how they did it. They came into my class, in front of everyone, and the nurse said, 'You have to come down to the office.' Now, at that point, everybody in the whole room knows what's going on. Every student in the class knew what was happening."

He reports that as soon as he arrived in the office, he was perceived to be guilty of drug use until he was able to give a test sample. He continues, "I didn't want to take the test, but I eventually did and passed it." The honor student claims the school's premise was this: "We're going to treat you as if you're guilty, and you're going to be tested again in five weeks."

The drug testing program has . . . unintended, negative consequences.

Rasmussen's high school began a program of mandatory **random** drug testing in 2008. The school's **policy** states that any student who participates in an **extracurricular** activity, club, or sport or who drives to school and parks on campus must submit to a drug test. The **method** consists of either mouth swabs or urine screenings administered by the school nurse.

From the beginning, Rasmussen opposed the principle of the tests and hesitated to participate in the program. However, he was a member of the National Honor Society, which made him part of the group of students required to take the tests. He realized that refusing to bc tcstcd would make him look guilty and possibly ruin his academic future.

"I'm not going to jeopardize myself as a competitive college applicant just to avoid a drug test," he says. "In previous years I was in school sports, now I'm in National Honor Society. It's not like I'm doing anything bad."

In fact, Rasmussen explains that the drug testing program has had several unintended, **negative** consequences. Some **individuals** have made poor choices just to avoid being caught in the net of the drug testing program.

"I know students who just won't do anything **extracurricular** at all because they do drugs," he says. "I know other people who have increased their drug use to drugs that are more dangerous, like moving from marijuana to cocaine and heroin just to pass the drug test because those drugs won't show up [on tests]."

Rasmussen notes that the Board listened to him but questions whether they really heard his point of view. He feels that the school district could be focusing on other issues than "picking out people for things they probably haven't done."

Loren Rasmussen voiced opposition to his school's mandatory drug testing program.

Positively Negative Results

by Doug Otero

"What's more important—doing drugs or doing your activities?" Sarah Pickus, a student at Green Valley High School in Clark County, Nevada, asks. For Pickus and over a thousand other students at the school, the answer is clear: "No" to drugs, and "Yes" to school activities.

Green Valley High School became the first public high school in Nevada to **randomly** test students for drug use in 2008. The program is still going strong. Students are getting **negative** results on drug tests, and the program is getting positive results from the school community.

Student Leah Yaffe sums up the positive attitude that many students have about **random** drug testing. "I don't see it as administrators trying to find out who the bad kids are," she says. "It's trying to find out who might have a problem."

Yaffe admits that the program may not be a **deterrent** for regular drug users, because they would avoid athletics or **extracurricular** activities in order not to be tested. However, she says that the testing program is a great excuse for kids who may be considering experimenting with drugs. Testing helps them say no to peer pressure and still save face.

Green Valley principal Jeff Horn began the program after the school caught eight student athletes using drugs and alcohol during the 2006–2007 school year. In 2008, during the school's first year of testing, seven student athletes tested positive. In the next year, the program proved itself. Zero student athletes tested positive.

Following Green Valley's lead, other high schools in the county are also adopting drug testing programs. In fact, mandatory **random** student drug testing is a growing trend across the nation. New Jersey, Florida, and Texas are among the states implementing this **policy** after the U.S. Supreme Court ruled that it is constitutional for athletes and students in **extracurricular** activities, such as choir, band, drama club, and student council.

Green Valley High School makes clear its **policy** on drug testing in this statement on its website: "The Administration, faculty and staff of Green Valley High School have the responsibility to keep all our students safe from drug abuse, a behavior that destroys bodies and minds, impedes academic and athletic performance, and creates barriers to success and happiness."

How do parents feel about the program? Principal Horn comments on **morale** at the school, "Our community is behind us." Students have a positive attitude as well. "Kids are not more nervous or scared, but I think they are more cautious," says Taylor Ashton, a sophomore. "And that's not only at school but on the weekends out of school."

Green Valley is passing all tests with flying colors. In 2010, *Newsweek* ranked it among the top high schools in the country.

Both students and officials at Green Valley High School believe the drug-testing policy has a positive impact on school morale.

Should parents have a say in how their teens use social media?

Across America, parents and their children are battling over teenagers' use of social media. Who's winning?

Parents as "Big Brother"

According to a recent Pew Research Center survey, 55% of American teens used social networking websites in 2006. In 2009, that number increased to 73%. This trend in social **communication** is shifting constantly. And many parents are **enforcing** their parental authority.

- 20% of the parents surveyed **control** their teens' use of social networks over privacy concerns.
- 72% **access** and monitor their teens' accounts. Half of the parents monitor weekly, and slightly over a third monitor daily.
- Overall, 88% of parents think their teens' privacy on social networks is important.

Reason for Caution

- 80% of the teens surveyed used privacy settings at some point to hide content from friends or parents.
- 42% accept social network "friend" requests from strangers.
- 31% share content, such as photos, that they do not want their family or teachers to see, on social networking sites.
- 18% have been embarrassed or disciplined for sharing something on a social network.

(Source: TRUSTe Social Networking and Privacy Survey, 2010)

Parents and Teens: Social Media Friends or Enemies?

by Lucy Tang-Lessing

The police chief of Mahwah, New Jersey, made headlines when he told parents on national television, "Steal Facebook passwords from your kids." Chief James Batelli says that most parents are naïve about what their teens are doing on the Internet. "Read the paper any day of the week and you'll see an abduction [or] a sexual assault that's the result of an Internet interaction or a Facebook comment," Batelli **cautions**. He advises parents to use spyware without telling their kids about it.

Dr. Jeffrey Kassinove, a family psychologist, disagrees. He says that spyware crosses a moral **boundary** and "sets up a situation of distrust." He points out, "First of all, you're encouraging your child that it's okay to lie because you're lying yourself, and you're conducting some secret action that they're not aware of."

A digital divide has sprung up in many households. On one side, parents want to monitor and **control** their teens' use of social media. On the other side, teenagers want privacy and independence. Can parents and teens ever be social media friends?

For today's parents and teens, social media is a source of constant battle.

Protection or Paranoia? ❶

Why do parents want to **control** how teens use social media? Many worry that the Internet is full of threatening people and other dangers. Their worst fear is that their children will become victims of online sexual predators by having **communication** with them through social media. Is this fear realistic, or is it paranoid?

Fourteen-year-old Jordan Glicksman describes how he started getting requests to be "friends" from adult strangers on a social networking site. "I don't know how that happened, and it was creepy," he says. Glicksman was smart enough to deny the requests. However, over 40% of online teens admit that they have friended strangers on social networking sites.

In 2006, a study by the Crimes Against Children Research Center **revealed** that one in five young people experience unwanted sexual solicitations through social media sites. Parents and public officials hit the panic button, concerned about their children's **security** online. In fact, most of the solicitations were from other kids. A governmental task force reported in 2009 that "the image presented by the media of an older male deceiving and preying on a young child does not paint an accurate picture of the nature of the majority of sexual solicitations and Internet-inspired offline encounters."

"My mom tried to 'friend' me, but I denied her request."

Still, nearly half of online teens visited MySpace and Facebook in May 2009, according to Nielsen, the media research and tracking company. And, a small but significant percentage of online encounters lead to exploitation of teens by adults. Many **cautious** parents are willing to use **censorship** to keep their child from being part of that statistic.

A Right to Privacy? ❷

In 2003, MySpace launched its social networking services, and by 2006 Facebook was offering **access** to anyone over the age of twelve. Millions of teens signed up. Their parents followed soon after.

Immediately, students formed a Facebook group called "Don't Let My Parents Onto Facebook!" Russell Taylor, a teen from Virginia, says, "My mom tried to 'friend' me, but I denied her request. I don't want my mom commenting on my pictures. That would be weird." Many teens try to **protect** their privacy from their parents by refusing to friend them or by using privacy settings to prohibit their parents' curious eyes.

Parents, however, feel that teens are using a double standard. Teens post information on their social networking pages that can be **accessed** by just about anyone with the right software. Employers, teachers, and college admissions officers regularly check Facebook profiles to research information about teens. "Kids

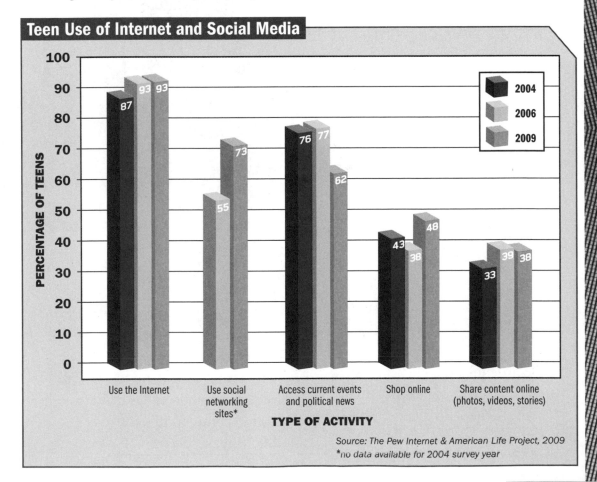

Teen Use of Internet and Social Media

Source: The Pew Internet & American Life Project, 2009
*no data available for 2004 survey year

shouldn't be putting anything inappropriate on Facebook anyway," says one anonymous parent. "It'll come back to haunt them in some way or another."

In addition, Internet advertisers **promote** their products and services to teen users who willingly give up credit card numbers, addresses, and other personal information. Scott Fitzsimones, 13, of Phoenix, Arizona, explains that a gaming app often requires him to **reveal** his location or personal information. If he doesn't click "OK," he can't continue to play. "I never say no," Fitzsimones admits. Like most teens, he willingly gives up his privacy on the Internet—just not to his parents.

A Matter of Trust? ❸

Anthony Orsini, a middle school principal in New Jersey, takes a hard line on social media. He advises parents to **enforce** a ban on social media. "There is absolutely, positively no reason for any middle school student to be part of a social networking site! None," Orsini **cautions**. He believes social networking has negative consequences for teens. "It doesn't help them to have more friends."

Without parental monitoring, certain aspects of social media may pose a threat to teens' safety.

A site selling software that **filters** and monitors Internet use encourages parents to **assume** the worst and spy on their kids. "It is a parent's job to watch over [their children] and be there to correct potential bad decisions that are all too common in a teenager's life," the site declares. Ten percent of parents admit to having login **access** to their children's social media accounts without their child's knowledge. Many more use software that prohibits their kids from going to certain Internet sites.

The privacy organization TRUSTe proposes a different approach: parents should not **censor** their children online. Instead, they should "trust, but verify." TRUSTe suggests that parents **assume** they can trust their kids, but check to see if that **assumption** is correct. Parents should ensure that teens are not accepting friend requests from strangers. TRUSTe also believes that both parents and teens have responsibilities regarding social media, including the responsibility to respect each other.

What about you? Are your parents friends—or enemies—in the world of social media?

Social Studies Content Connection

The Facebook Revolution

In 2011, change swept across the Arab world as demonstrators protested against their governments in countries like Tunisia, Egypt, and Libya.

The Plan: Young Egyptians seeking democracy used a new weapon—social media—to launch the revolution. They created a Facebook "event" and scheduled a peaceful gathering in Cairo's Tahrir Square.

The Event: Almost instantly, over 80,000 people accepted the January 25th invitation named "The Day of Revolution Against Torture, Poverty, Corruption and Unemployment."

The Result: President Hosni Mubarak, the dictator of Egypt for 30 years, eventually resigned from office.

The Quote: During the protests, one Cairo activist posted this famous quote on Twitter: "We use Facebook to schedule protests, Twitter to coordinate, and YouTube to tell the world."

Take a Stand

Should governments monitor how citizens use social media? Why or why not?

Harlan Coben: Parent Spy

by Marisol Diaz

Harlan Coben is a best-selling author of mysteries and thrillers with about 50 million books in print around the world. He is also the parent of four children, some of them in their "tweens" or teens. Many of Coben's books are set in his native New Jersey where his characters, often teenagers, get caught up in heart-pounding plots involving drugs, blackmail, murder—and the Internet.

One novel, titled *Hold Tight*, is about a teen whose parents use spyware to monitor his social media accounts. What they learn from their spying is chilling—for both the parents and the boy. Many readers wondered if Coben, known as an all-around nice guy, thought parents should spy on their children's online activities. To their surprise, he answered without hesitation, "It's scary. But a good idea."

Coben admits that "spyware" is a word that makes him think of government officials trying to read people's thoughts. In fact, the invasion of someone's privacy seems downright un-American. However, he emphasizes, the Internet is not private anyway. "Everything your child types can already be seen by the world—teachers, potential

Harlan Coben argues that parents should control their teens' use of social media.

employers, friends, neighbors, future dates. Shouldn't [a teen] learn now that the Internet is not a haven of privacy?"

> **Spyware revealed to one of Coben's friends that his daughter was using drugs and having a relationship with her dealer.**

Coben believes that trust is essential between parents and teens. However, he is also a believer in parental responsibility, especially concerning technology that gives the entire world **access** to your home. He expressed his opinions in an article titled "The Undercover Parent" in *The New York Times*.

"Today's overprotective parents fight their kids' battles on the playground, berate coaches about playing time, and fill out college applications. Yet, when it comes to chatting with pedophiles or watching beheadings or gambling away their entire life savings, then . . . their children deserve independence?"

Does Coben think spying on teenagers' social media activities is enjoyable? Absolutely not. In fact, he says that not spying is the easy way out. It's tough for parents to learn about what goes on in chat rooms, to read the cruel comments of cyberbullies, and to find out that their **assumptions** about their teens might be wrong. For example, spyware **revealed** to one of Coben's friends that his daughter was using drugs and having a relationship with her dealer.

Should parents tell their children that they are spying on them? Coben says that, for him, the answer is yes. Some **boundaries** must be crossed to **protect** your child. He emphasizes that there is one thing that technology can never replace— honest **communication** between parents and their children.

A Family United Against Spying

by Lincoln Beyer

How would the members of a family feel about parents spying on their children's Facebook accounts? You might **assume** that no five members of a family could agree on this issue—especially a family with teenage kids. Your **assumption** would be incorrect. This family not only shares **communication**, they share the same values when it comes to social media and parental **control**.

In the online magazine, *Your Teen*, a "virtual family" of bloggers—a dad, mom, college daughter, high school son, and junior high son—commented on this issue that many families with teens face. The members of this virtual family are not related in real life. However, they are real people, and they are an actual mother, father, college-age daughter, and two teenage sons.

The following are excerpts from the virtual family's blog.

Mindy, mother of three teenagers:

"Dad and I have never checked your text messages or your Facebook accounts. When this discussion comes up with our friends, it seems that most parents are checking and they think we are crazy because we don't. Would it be easier for you to resist the temptation to put certain things on Facebook if you knew we were checking?"

Devan, a college sophomore:

"I think that when parents go on their children's Facebook pages and look on their phones, it is a complete invasion of privacy. I am sure you would be upset if I looked at your phone or at your emails or any personal messages. Looking at diaries, notes, Facebook pages, MySpace pages, emails, AIMs, text messages, is the equivalent of spying, and it's not okay."

Dan, father of three teenagers:

"Even if I knew how to check your Facebook posts, tweets, and texts, I wouldn't do it. I also wouldn't read your diary, or snoop around your room when you're not home. I trust you, and respect your privacy. The only thing is . . . trust is a two-way street. If at some point you started lying to us or deceiving us, then we would lose that trust."

"I think that when parents go on their children's Facebook pages and look on their phones, it is a complete invasion of privacy."

Amnon, 18, a high school senior:

"I feel that checking texts and Facebook is not the right way to go. First of all, privacy is one of the most important freedoms in a person's life. I believe the most effective thing for parents to do is to warn their kids by making clear exactly how easy it is to fall into an online, life-ruining trap. The dangers are real, and kids need to be aware of the potential outcomes."

Ryan, 13, an eighth-grade student:

"If I'm texting someone, and I know my parents are checking my messages, then yeah I probably won't say the stuff I would say if my parents weren't checking. For example, I'd say "stinks" instead of "sucks," or not swear when I'm really mad. However, it might make me feel uncomfortable when talking to someone, for example a girl or a girlfriend. If nothing inappropriate is said, and it's just talking, I don't want my parents snooping into my social life."

These "family members" all say "No" to Facebook snooping. Do you think most families would share the same perspective?

ACADEMIC LANGUAGE HANDBOOK

Use the academic language frames in this handbook as a reference during academic discussions.

The **heading** states the overall type of discussion or interaction.

Look for the **"If" statement** that most closely describes the specific type of interaction.

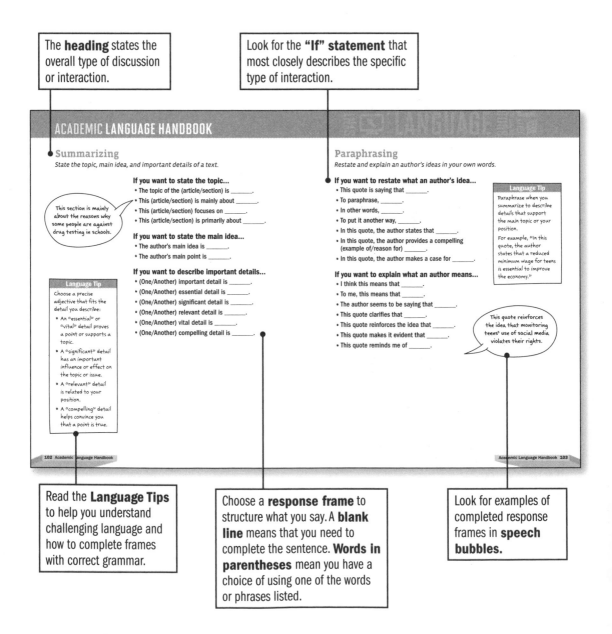

ACADEMIC LANGUAGE HANDBOOK

Summarizing
State the topic, main idea, and important details of a text.

If you want to state the topic...
- The topic of the (article/section) is _____.
- This (article/section) is mainly about _____.
- This (article/section) focuses on _____.
- This (article/section) is primarily about _____.

> This section is mainly about the reasons why some people are against drug testing in schools.

If you want to state the main idea...
- The author's main idea is _____.
- The author's main point is _____.

If you want to describe important details...
- (One/Another) important detail is _____.
- (One/Another) essential detail is _____.
- (One/Another) significant detail is _____.
- (One/Another) relevant detail is _____.
- (One/Another) vital detail is _____.
- (One/Another) compelling detail is _____.

Language Tip

Choose a precise adjective that fits the detail you describe:
- An "essential" or "vital" detail proves a point or supports a topic.
- A "significant" detail has an important influence or effect on the topic or issue.
- A "relevant" detail is related to your position.
- A "compelling" detail helps convince you that a point is true.

Paraphrasing
Restate and explain an author's ideas in your own words.

If you want to restate what an author's idea...
- This quote is saying that _____.
- To paraphrase, _____.
- In other words, _____.
- To put it another way, _____.
- In this quote, the author states that _____.
- In this quote, the author provides a compelling (example of/reason for) _____.
- In this quote, the author makes a case for _____.

If you want to explain what an author means...
- I think this means that _____.
- To me, this means that _____.
- The author seems to be saying that _____.
- This quote clarifies that _____.
- This quote reinforces the idea that _____.
- This quote makes it evident that _____.
- This quote reminds me of _____.

Language Tip

Paraphrase when you summarize to describe details that support the main topic or your position.
For example, "In this quote, the author states that a reduced minimum wage for teens is essential to improve the economy."

> This quote reinforces the idea that monitoring teens' use of social media violates their rights.

Read the **Language Tips** to help you understand challenging language and how to complete frames with correct grammar.

Choose a **response frame** to structure what you say. A **blank line** means that you need to complete the sentence. **Words in parentheses** mean you have a choice of using one of the words or phrases listed.

Look for examples of completed response frames in **speech bubbles.**

Requesting Assistance

Ask the teacher or a classmate for help.

If you don't understand what the speaker said...
- I couldn't hear you. Could you repeat that?
- I didn't hear you completely. Please repeat that.

If you don't understand what the speaker meant...
- I don't quite understand. Could you give me an example?
- I am somewhat confused. Could you explain that again?
- I am not sure I get your point. Could you run that by me again?

> **Language Tip**
>
> The idiom "run that by me again" means "explain it to me again in a different way."

Asking for Clarification

Ask for more information.

If you have a question...
- I have a question about _____.
- One question I have is _____.

If you need information repeated...
- Will you explain _____ again?

If you need more explanation...
- What do you mean by _____?
- I don't quite understand _____.
- What exactly do you mean by _____?
- Could you explain what you mean by _____?

Will you explain the directions for this activity again?

What exactly do you mean by "the topic sentence"?

Discussing Word Knowledge

Talk about how well you know a specific word.

No. I have never heard the word "biased."

Language Tip

Follow "has something to do with..." with a noun or verb phrase that you associate with the word.

For example, "We think disposable has something to do with throwing away trash."

If you want to ask someone about a word...

- Are you familiar with the word _____?

If you don't know the word...

- No. I have never heard the word _____.

If you recognize the word...

- I recognize _____. It has something to do with _____.
- We would benefit from a review of the word _____.

If you are familiar with the word...

- We have some understanding of the word _____.
- We think _____ (means/has to do with) _____.

If you know the word...

- I know the word _____. It means _____.
- I can use _____ in a sentence. For example, _____.

Stating Perspectives

Give your opinion about an issue or a topic.

If you want to share your opinion...

- I think that _____.
- I (firmly) believe that _____.
- In my opinion, _____.
- From my perspective, _____.
- From my point of view, _____.
- I would argue that _____.
- I have observed that _____.
- I imagine that _____.
- Considering _____, my stance is that _____.
- Due to _____, I _____.
- Based on my experience as a(n) _____, _____.
- Based on my experience with (verb + *-ing*) _____, _____.

> **Language Tip**
>
> Follow these response frames with a noun phrase that gives your opinion.
>
> For example, "I would argue that graffiti is vandalism."

> Based on my experience as a teen, I believe that images in the media can harm teens' self-image.

> **Language Tip**
>
> Some frames require verb phrases in addition to noun phrases.
>
> For example, "Based on my experience with playing on a basketball team, I believe that girls can be as competitive as boys."

Introducing Evidence

Provide supporting evidence for your claim.

If you want to give text evidence...

- For (example/instance), _____.
- To illustrate, _____.
- As an illustration, _____.
- In the article, _____.
- The article (also) _____.
- In addition, the article _____.
- The author (also) _____.
- The data (show/prove) _____.
- Studies (show/prove) _____.
- Recent findings (show/prove) _____.

If you want to give evidence from experience...

- In my experience, _____.
- Based on my experience, _____.
- Drawing from my (family life/experience), _____.
- In my school experience, _____.
- Within my (culture/community), _____.
- Among my (peers/classmates), _____.
- As a(n) (athlete/student/_____), _____.
- Based on my experience as a(n) _____, _____.
- Based on my experience with (verb + *-ing*) _____, _____.

> Based on my experience as a child of a diabetic, I have learned that unhealthy food increases a person's risk of developing the disease.

Discussing With Others

Participate in a group or class discussion.

If you want to ask a group member to respond...
- Who would like to share first?
- We haven't heard from you yet.
- What are your thoughts?
- Does anyone have anything to add?

If you want to hold the floor...
- As I was saying, _____.
- Can I add an idea?
- What I was trying to say was _____.
- If I could finish my thought, _____.
- I'd like to complete my thought.

Language Tip
"Hold the floor" is an idiom that means "keep the attention of the listeners."

If you want to interject an idea...
- May I (say/add) an idea?
- I have another idea.
- I'd like to offer another perspective.

Language Tip
To interject politely, wait for a pause in the discussion rather than speaking at the same time as someone else.

If you want to report a partner's idea...
- [Name] shared with me that _____.
- [Name] pointed out to me that _____.
- [Name] (indicated/emphasized) that _____.

Kendra pointed out to me that just because animals can't speak doesn't mean that they don't experience pain.

If you want to report a group's idea...
- We (decided/agreed) that _____.
- We (determined/concluded) that _____.
- Our group sees it differently.
- We had a different approach.

Restating Ideas

Listen carefully and repeat classmates' ideas in your own words.

If you want to restate someone else's idea...

* So you think that _____.
* So what you're (saying/suggesting) is that _____.
* So your (opinion/perspective) is that _____.
* In other words, you have observed that _____.
* In other words, your (point of view/stance) is that _____.
* So if I understand you correctly, your (opinion/ perspective) is that _____.

If someone restates your idea correctly...

* Yes, that's right.
* Yes, that's correct.
* Yes, that's accurate.

> Actually, what I meant was people can adjust to using reusable bags instead of plastic bags.

If someone restates your idea incorrectly...

* No, not really. What I meant was _____.
* Actually, what I meant was _____.
* No, not exactly. What I meant was _____.
* No, not quite. What I meant was _____.
* No. What I intended to say was _____.

Drawing Conclusions

Report evidence and explain what you know to be true about it.

If you want to report data or statistics...

- A piece of data that caught my attention is that _____.
- One surprising statistic is that _____.

> One surprising statistic is that nearly 7,000 high school students drop out every day in this country.

If you want to state a conclusion...

- The evidence leads me to conclude that _____.
- The data suggest that _____.
- Based on _____, I assume that _____.
- After reading, I conclude that _____.
- For these reasons, I (maintain/conclude) that _____.
- Therefore, I (conclude/remain convinced) that _____.

Language Tip
When you "maintain" a position, you strongly express that your position is true.

Comparing Ideas

Discuss how your ideas are similar to or different from others' ideas.

If you agree with an idea...

- I agree with _____'s idea.
- I agree with _____'s (opinion/perspective).
- I completely agree with _____'s (opinion/perspective).
- I agree with _____'s point of view about _____.
- I see it the same way as _____.

> I agree with Lydia's point of view about banning junk food in schools.

If you disagree with an idea...

- I don't quite agree with _____'s idea.
- I disagree with _____'s point of view about _____.
- I disagree with _____'s (opinion/perspective).
- I completely disagree with _____'s (opinion/perspective).
- I disagree with _____'s point of view about _____.

If your idea is similar...

- My (experience/belief) is similar to _____'s.
- My perspective on _____ is similar to _____'s.
- My observation is similar to _____'s.
- My stance is similar to _____'s.
- My point of view is related to _____'s.

Language Tip
Your "observation" about a topic is something you have noticed about it. Your "stance" on an issue is your position.

If your idea is different...

- My belief is different from _____'s.
- My perspective on _____ is different from _____'s.
- My observation is different from _____'s.
- My stance is different from _____'s.
- I see it a different way than _____ does.

My perspective on whether scientists should be able to use animals for research is different from Rob's.

If you are undecided about an idea...

- I'm undecided about _____'s idea.
- I'm uncertain about _____'s idea.
- I'm unconvinced about _____'s idea.
- I'm unsure about _____'s idea.
- I see both sides of the issue.
- I can't definitively agree or disagree with _____'s idea.
- I am undecided whether _____.
- I am more inclined to believe that _____.
- I remain unconvinced that _____.
- I need to consider the idea of _____ further.

Language Tip

When you "definitively" agree or disagree with something, your opinion cannot be changed.

Summarizing

State the topic, main idea, and important details of a text.

This section is mainly about the reasons why some people are against drug testing in schools.

If you want to state the topic...
- The topic of the (article/section) is _____.
- This (article/section) is mainly about _____.
- This (article/section) focuses on _____.
- This (article/section) is primarily about _____.

If you want to state the main idea...
- The author's main idea is _____.
- The author's main point is _____.

If you want to describe important details...
- (One/Another) important detail is _____.
- (One/Another) essential detail is _____.
- (One/Another) significant detail is _____.
- (One/Another) relevant detail is _____.
- (One/Another) vital detail is _____.
- (One/Another) compelling detail is _____.

Language Tip

Choose a precise adjective that fits the detail you describe:

- An "essential" or "vital" detail proves a point or supports a topic.
- A "significant" detail has an important influence or effect on the topic or issue.
- A "relevant" detail is related to your position.
- A "compelling" detail helps convince you that a point is true.

Paraphrasing

Restate and explain an author's ideas in your own words.

If you want to restate an author's idea...

- This quote is saying that _____.
- To paraphrase, _____.
- In other words, _____.
- To put it another way, _____.
- In this quote, the author states that _____.
- In this quote, the author provides a compelling (example of/reason for) _____.
- In this quote, the author makes a case for _____.

If you want to explain what an author means...

- I think this means that _____.
- To me, this means that _____.
- The author seems to be saying that _____.
- This quote clarifies that _____.
- This quote reinforces the idea that _____.
- This quote makes it evident that _____.
- This quote reminds me of _____.

> **Language Tip**
>
> Paraphrase when you summarize to describe details that support the main topic or your position.
>
> For example, "In this quote, the author states that a reduced minimum wage for teens is essential to improve the economy."

This quote reinforces the idea that monitoring teens' use of social media violates their rights.

Responding to Text

Use these frames to share your response to a statement or quote.

If you agree or disagree...

- I agree with this (statement/quote).
- I disagree with this (statement/quote).
- This (statement/quote) contradicts my (opinion/perspective).
- This (statement/quote) supports my (opinion/perspective).

If a statement gets your attention...

- I noticed this (statement/quote) also.
- This (statement/quote) stood out for me.
- This (statement/quote) caught my attention.
- This (statement/quote) took me by surprise.
- This (statement/quote) made me curious about (noun phrase) _____.

If you can relate...

- This (statement/quote) reminded me of my experiences.
- This (statement/quote) reminded me of my experience as (noun phrase) _____.
- This (statement/quote) concerned me as a (noun/noun phrase) _____.
- This (statement/quote) reminded me of (verb + *-ing*) _____.
- This (statement/quote) resonated with me.
- This (statement/quote) validates my experience.

This statement made me curious about funding for girls' sports.

This quote reminded me of my experience as a female athlete.

If you have a positive response...

- This (statement/quote) interested me.
- This (statement/quote) surprised me.
- This (statement/quote) impressed me.
- This (statement/quote) intrigued me.
- This (statement/quote) fascinated me.
- I found this (statement/quote) interesting.
- I found this (statement/quote) surprising.
- I found this (statement/quote) impressive.
- I found this (statement/quote) intriguing.
- I found this (statement/quote) fascinating.

If you have a negative response...

- This (statement/quote) bothered me.
- This (statement/quote) shocked me.
- This (statement/quote) concerned me.
- This (statement/quote) alarmed me.
- This (statement/quote) astonished me.
- I found this (statement/quote) troubling.
- I found this (statement/quote) shocking.
- I found this (statement/quote) concerning.
- I found this (statement/quote) alarming.
- I found this (statement/quote) astonishing.

Language Tip
If you have the same response as someone else, state your response and add "as well" to the end.
For example, "This statement interested me as well."

Language Tip
If you start your response with "I found this (statement/quote)...," complete it with an adjective that ends with "–ing."
For example, "I found this statement shocking."

Affirming Ideas

Acknowledge a classmate's idea before stating your own idea.

If you want to acknowledge others' ideas...

- That's an interesting claim.
- I hadn't thought of that.
- That's an interesting opinion.
- I see what you mean.
- I can understand why you see it this way.
- That's an intriguing perspective.
- That's a compelling point of view.

Language Tip

Acknowledge that a classmate had something valuable to say. Then use a transition such as "however" or "I also think" to state your own perspective.

For example, "I see what you mean. However, I believe that advertisements present images that often harm teens' self-esteem."

Some students may miss school for health reasons, rather than because they are skipping school. It's not fair to punish those students by withholding their driver's licenses.

I hadn't thought of that.

Offering Feedback

Share your feedback and suggestions about a classmate's writing or speech.

If you want to give positive feedback...

- You did an effective job of organizing _____.
- You did an effective job of including _____.
- You did an effective job of stating _____.
- I appreciate how you used _____.
- I appreciate how you included _____.
- I appreciate your effort to (organize/include/state) _____.
- I appreciate your use of _____.
- I appreciate your skillful _____.

> ### Language Tip
>
> Complete the frames to give positive feedback with a noun phrase.
>
> For example, "You did an effective job of stating reasons why you think schools should be responsible for punishing cyberbullies."

If you want to offer a suggestion...

- Your (writing/speech) _____ would be stronger if you _____.
- As you revise your (writing/speech) _____, focus on _____.
- As you revise your (writing/speech) _____, make a point of _____.

As you revise your argument, make a point of including evidence from the article to support your claim.

ACADEMIC GLOSSARY

A glossary is a useful tool found at the back of many books. It contains information about key words in the text. Review the sample glossary entry below.

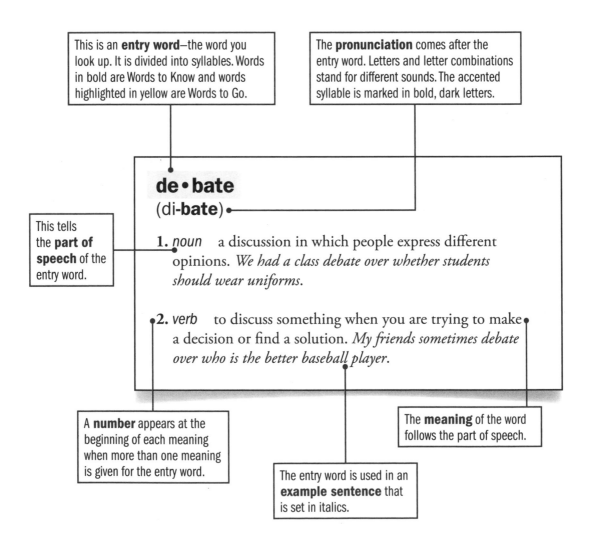

This is an **entry word**—the word you look up. It is divided into syllables. Words in bold are Words to Know and words highlighted in yellow are Words to Go.

The **pronunciation** comes after the entry word. Letters and letter combinations stand for different sounds. The accented syllable is marked in bold, dark letters.

This tells the **part of speech** of the entry word.

de•bate
(di-**bate**)

1. *noun*   a discussion in which people express different opinions. *We had a class debate over whether students should wear uniforms.*

2. *verb*   to discuss something when you are trying to make a decision or find a solution. *My friends sometimes debate over who is the better baseball player.*

A **number** appears at the beginning of each meaning when more than one meaning is given for the entry word.

The **meaning** of the word follows the part of speech.

The entry word is used in an **example sentence** that is set in italics.

a•bil•i•ty
(uh-**bil**-i-tee)

noun   something that a person can do. *Superman is a fictional character who has the ability to fly.*

ac•cess
(**ak**-sess)

noun   the ability to use or enter a place. *The employees use ID cards to gain access to the office building.*

ac•count•a•ble
(uh-**kount**-uh-buhl)

adjective   responsible for your actions and the effects they have. *As a babysitter, I am accountable for keeping the children I'm watching safe and entertained.*

a•chieve
(uh-**cheev**)

verb   to succeed in accomplishing the result you want. *The singer worked hard to achieve her goal of receiving an American Music Award.*

ad•dic•tion
(uh-**dik**-shuhn)

noun   the physical or emotional need to do something that is harmful on a regular basis. *My dad is trying to quit smoking and break his addiction to cigarettes.*

ad•dic•tive
(uh-**dik**-tiv)

adjective   hard to give up. *Some prescription drugs are so addictive that people need help to stop taking them.*

af•fect
(uh-**fekt**)

verb   to change someone or something; to make someone have strong feelings. *Music has the power to affect people no matter what language they speak.*

ag•gres•sive
(uh-**gress**-iv)

adjective   powerful and wanting to win. *The coach asked Sue to play offense on the team because she is fearless and aggressive.*

al•ter•na•tive
(awl-**tur**-nuh-tiv)

1. *adjective*   offering a different way, plan, or idea as a choice. *The cafeteria offers alternative meals for people who don't eat meat.*

2. *noun*   something chosen instead of something else. *You should consider every alternative before making a major decision like changing schools.*

an•ti so•cial
(an-tee **soh**-shuhl)

adjective   not interested in spending time with other people. *People think my brother is anti-social, but he's really just shy.*

ACADEMIC GLOSSARY

ap•peal
(uh-**peel**)
verb to be likeable or interesting. *Roland could become our next student council president since his message appeals to students in all grades.*

ap•peal•ing
(uh-**peel**-ing)
adjective likeable or interesting. *Action films make a lot of money at the box office because many people find them appealing.*

ap•pear•ance
(uh-**peer**-uhnss)
noun the way that people and objects look or seem. *Because she's worried about what friends will think about her new haircut, Sara often checks her appearance in the mirror.*

ap•proach
(uh-**prohch**)
noun a way of dealing with something. *Yelling did not quiet the class, so Mr. Wu tried a different approach.*

ap•pro•pri•ate
(uh-**proh**-pree-uht)
adjective suitable or correct for a situation. *Jeans and sneakers are not appropriate to wear to the prom.*

ar•gue
(**ar**-gyoo)
verb to state an opinion. *The politician tried to argue that video games harm teens, but most people don't believe that.*

ar•gu•ment
(**ar**-gyoo-muhnt)
noun the statement of an opinion. *During a talk with my dad, I made the argument that getting a weekly allowance would teach me how to manage money.*

ar•tis•tic
(ar-**tiss**-tik)
adjective good at drawing or painting; done with skill and imagination. *The art teacher liked my drawing and told me I was very artistic.*

as•pect
(**ass**-pekt)
noun one of the parts of a situation, plan, or idea. *Our favorite aspect of summer break is visiting family in Mexico.*

as•sume
(uh-**soom**)
verb to think that something is true without having definite proof. *Since you're wearing shorts, I assume it's hot outside today.*

as•sump•tion
(uh-**suhmp**-shuhn)
noun a belief that something is true without having definite proof. *Justin's older sister was driving, so I made the assumption that she had a driver's license.*

ath•lete
(**ath**-leet)
noun someone who is trained in or very good at sports. *Oscar is a talented athlete who can play five different sports.*

ath•let•ic
(ath-**let**-ik)

adjective able to play sports well. *I'm not very athletic, so I joined the drama club instead of trying out for the soccer team.*

at•tend
(uh-**tend**)

verb to go to or be present at a meeting, class, or other gathering. *My mom tries to attend all my parent-teacher meetings to stay informed about my grades.*

at•ten•dance
(uh-**ten**-duhns)

noun the act of going to or being present in class, at a meeting, or at another gathering. *Your regular attendance at play rehearsals is important since you have the lead role.*

au•thor•i•ty
(uh-**thor**-uh-tee)

noun the official right or power to tell others what to do. *The principal used her authority to cancel our afternoon classes.*

a•vail•a•ble
(uh-**vayl**-uh-buhl)

adjective possible to get or be used; not busy, or unoccupied. *Our teacher is available after school if we need extra help.*

ban
(**ban**)

1. *verb* to say that something must not be allowed to happen. *School officials want to ban junk food from the vending machines at school.*

2. *noun* an important public pronouncement saying that something must not be allowed to happen. *The mayor plans to announce a ban on smoking at bus stops.*

ben•e•fi•cial
(ben-uh-**fish**-uhl)

adjective having a good or helpful effect on something. *Regular exercise is beneficial to teens' health.*

ben•e•fit
(**ben**-uh-fit)

1. *verb* to help or be helped by something or someone. *Everyone could benefit from getting a good night's sleep and drinking plenty of water.*

2. *noun* something that is helpful or good for you. *One benefit of riding my bike to school is that I get there before the bus.*

bi•as
(**bye**-uhs)

noun an opinion about whether a person, group, or idea is good or bad. *My friend has an unfair bias about the people who live on the other side of town.*

bi•ased
(**bye**-uhst)

adjective favoring one person or group over another in an unfair way. *Lisa is biased against the new student because he comes from another country.*

bound•a•ry
(**boun**-duh-ree)

noun the limit of what is possible or acceptable. *The new rule set a boundary for what students can wear to school dances.*

cal•o•rie
(**kal**-uh-ree)

noun a unit of energy produced by food. *If you're trying to lose weight, every calorie counts toward reaching your goal.*

ca•pa•ble
(**kay**-puh-buhl)

adjective having the ability to do something. *My favorite comic book character is capable of seeing through walls.*

cau•tion
(**kaw**-shun)

noun the state of being careful about avoiding danger or trouble. *You must use caution when cooking a meal.*

cau•tious
(**kaw**-shuhss)

adjective careful about avoiding danger or trouble. *A cautious bicyclist always wears a helmet when riding.*

cen•sor
(**sen**-sur)

verb to remove anything considered offensive or dangerous from a work of art or other text. *Some radio stations censor music they believe is bad for young audiences.*

cen•sor•ship
(**sen**-sur-ship)

noun the act of removing anything considered offensive or dangerous from a book, film, or work of art. *Tia is a firm believer in censorship when it comes to scary movies!*

cir•cum•stan•ces
(**sur**-kuhm-stan-ssez)

noun conditions or facts that are connected to a situation or event. *We are allowed to use those exits only under emergency circumstances.*

civ•il lib•er•ties
(**siv**-il **lib**-ur-teez)

noun the rights of all people, such as their freedom of speech. *Even though I'm under 18, I still have civil liberties that adults should not take for granted.*

com•mu•ni•ca•tion
(kuh-myoo-nuh-**kay**-shuhn)

noun the act of sharing information or expressing thoughts and feelings. *My cell phone helps me stay in constant communication with my friends.*

com·mu·ni·ty
(kuh-**myoo**-nuh-tee)

noun   a group of people who live in an area; the area where a group of people live. *My community sponsors a music festival every summer.*

com·pen·sa·tion
(kom-puhn-**say**-shuhn)

noun   the payment a person receives for working at a job. *My mom switched jobs because the new one offers better compensation.*

com·pete
(kuhm-**peet**)

verb   to try to do better than others at a task, game, or contest. *Every year, I compete in the school spelling bee.*

com·pe·ti·tion
(kom-puh-**tish**-uhn)

noun   a task, game, or contest in which there is a winner. *My friends and I had a competition to see who could read the most books in a month.*

con·cern
(kuhn-**surn**)

noun   a feeling of worry about something important. *My track coach showed concern when I failed to complete the race.*

con·fi·den·tial
(kon-fuh-**den**-shuhl)

adjective   meant to be kept secret. *Our teacher told us that all of our test scores would be kept confidential.*

con·se·quence
(kon-suh-**kwenss**)

noun   something that happens because of an action. *The A on my report card is a direct consequence of the studying I did.*

con·sum·er
(kuhn-**soo**-mur)

noun   someone who buys or uses products and services. *That store offers consumers a discount if they are shopping there for the first time.*

con·tact sport
(**kon**-takt **sport**)

noun   a game in which players often hit or bump into each other. *It is important to wear a helmet while playing a contact sport, like hockey, to avoid injury.*

con·trib·ute
(kuhn-**trib**-yoot)

verb   to help make something happen. *If we want the bake sale to be successful, we all have to contribute an item to sell.*

con·trol
(kuhn-**trohl**)

verb   to make someone or something do what you want. *My mom can't control us whenever we're at the park.*

con·tro·ver·sy
(**kon**-truh-vur-see)

noun   a serious disagreement among many people. *The teacher's decision to cancel the field trip caused a controversy among students.*

ACADEMIC GLOSSARY

co•or•di•na•tion
(ko-or-dih-**nay**-shuhn)

noun   the ability to use parts of the body or other items so that they work together. *Circus performers need excellent coordination to juggle dangerous objects.*

crit•i•cism
(**krit**-uh-siz-uhm)

noun   remarks that say what you think is bad about someone or something. *After we gave our presentation, the teacher offered some helpful criticism.*

cri•tique
(kri-**teek**)

noun   a collection of remarks that say what you think is bad about someone or something. *Leon wrote a critique of the new movie for the school newspaper.*

cru•el
(**kroo**-uhl)

adjective   purposely causing suffering and pain. *Some people think testing products on animals is cruel.*

cul•tur•al
(**kuhl**-chur-uhl)

adjective   having to do with the art, ideas, and beliefs of a group of people. *During Cultural Appreciation Day, I learned about the customs of classmates from different countries.*

da•ta
(**day**-tuh)

noun   information or facts. *We gathered data about the weather in science class.*

de•bate
(di-**bate**)

1. *noun*   a discussion in which people express different opinions. *We had a class debate over whether students should wear uniforms.*

2. *verb*   to discuss something when you are trying to make a decision or find a solution. *My friends sometimes debate over who is the better baseball player.*

de•face
(di-**fayss**)

verb   to destroy or damage the way something looks. *It is a crime to deface other people's property.*

de•ter
(di-**tur**)

verb   to keep something from happening by threatening an unpleasant result. *The terrible weather forecast will not deter me from going to the amusement park.*

de•ter•rent
(di-**tur**-uhnt)

noun   something that is meant to keep something from happening. *A $500 fine is an effective deterrent against littering.*

dis•crim•i•nate
(diss-**krim**-uh-nate)

verb   to treat people differently from others in an unfair way. *People concerned with civil rights try to educate people who discriminate against minorities.*

dis•crim•i•na•tion
(diss-krim-i-**nay**-shuhn)

noun   the practice of treating people differently from others in an unfair way. *Not allowing boys to join the cheerleading team is a form of discrimination.*

dis•or•der
(diss-**or**-dur)

noun   an illness or condition. *Many schools have special programs for students with learning disorders.*

dis•pos•a•ble
(dis-**poh**-zuh-buhl)

adjective   designed to be used briefly and thrown away. *We used disposable bags for the cleanup so that everything could be thrown away.*

dis•tract
(diss-**trakt**)

verb   to take a person's attention away from someone or something. *We tried not to let the barking dog distract us from our homework.*

dis•trac•tion
(diss-**trakt**-shuhn)

noun   something that takes a person's attention away from someone or something. *Talking on a cell phone while driving can be a dangerous distraction.*

di•verse
(dye-**vurss**)

adjective   very different from one another. *A well-rounded student has many diverse interests.*

di•ver•si•ty
(di-**vur**-sih-tee)

noun   a variety. *I see a lot of diversity in the clothes that the designer makes.*

earn
(**urn**)

verb   to make money by working at a job. *I babysat for my neighbors so that I could earn money for a new MP3 player.*

earn•ings
(**ur**-nings)

noun   the money that a person receives for the work he or she does. *I can't believe my sister spent a month's earnings on shoes!*

e•co•nom•ic
(ehk-uh-**nom**-ik)

adjective   of or relating to the system by which money and goods are produced and used within a country or area. *We've been learning about China's economic policies in social studies class.*

e•con•o•my
(ee-**kon**-uh-mee)

noun   the system by which money and goods are produced and used within a country or area. *My family shops at local stores to help support the local economy.*

em•ploy
(em-**ploi**)

verb   to pay someone to work at a job. *The owner of the ice cream store wants to employ a student to work part-time.*

ACADEMIC GLOSSARY

em•ploy•ment
(em-**ploi**-mehnt)
noun the condition of working at a job. *John needs money to buy a new phone, so he is looking for employment.*

en•force
(en-**forss**)
verb to make people obey a rule or law. *My parents enforce my curfew, so I need to be home by 9:00 P.M.*

en•sure
(en-**shur**)
verb to make certain that something will happen properly. *The only way that you can ensure you will do well on the test is to study for it.*

en•ter•tain•ment
(en-tur-**tayn**-mehnt)
noun something people watch or do to enjoy themselves. *Board games are good entertainment for both kids and adults.*

en•vi•ron•ment
(en-**vye**-ruhn-muhnt)
noun the land, water, and air in which people, plants, and animals live. *In order to help the environment, I always try to pick up any trash I see on the ground.*

ep•i•dem•ic
(ep-uh-**dem**-ik)
noun a sudden outbreak of a disease or other bad condition that spreads quickly. *Every winter the flu epidemic hits our school and forces many students to stay home.*

es•ti•mate
(**ess**-ti-mate)
1. *verb* to guess the size, speed, or amount of something. *To win the prize, we had to estimate how many jelly beans were in the jar.*

(**ess**-ti-muht)
2. *noun* a guess about the size, speed, or amount of something. *After everyone had made an estimate, the person who came closest to the actual amount won.*

ev•i•dence
(**ev**-uh-duhnss)
noun facts, information, or signs that show that something is true. *The fact that I got a perfect score on the test is evidence that I understand the material.*

ex•pense
(ek-**spenss**)
noun money spent on a particular thing. *We made a list of each expense to see exactly what we spent our money on.*

ex•pen•sive
(ek-**spen**-siv)
adjective costing a lot of money. *Amy had to mow two dozen lawns to earn enough money for her expensive new jacket.*

ex•per•i•ment
(ek-**sper**-uh-ment)

1. *noun* a scientific test to try out an idea or to see the effect of something. *In science class, we did an experiment to see if plants could grow without light.*

2. *verb* to try out an idea or to see the effect of something. *The scientist wanted to experiment with different medicines to see which ones would best help sick people.*

ex•pose
(ek-**spoze**)

verb to give someone the chance to experience something. *Our teacher tries to expose us to many different kinds of cultures through the stories we read.*

ex•po•sure
(ek-**spoh**-zhur)

noun the chance to experience something. *Too much exposure to the sun without sunscreen could damage your skin.*

ex•press
(ek-**spress**)

verb to tell or show what you are thinking or feeling with words, looks, or actions. *I like to express my feelings by drawing pictures.*

ex•pres•sion
(ek-**spresh**-uhn)

noun the act of telling or showing what you are thinking or feeling with words, looks, or actions. *The expression on David's face showed that he was completely surprised by the party.*

ex•tra•cur•ri•cu•lar
(ek-struh-kur-**ik**-yoo-luhr)

adjective not part of the regular course schedule at school. *I take piano lessons as an extracurricular activity.*

fil•ter
(**fil**-tur)

verb to use a computer program to block a website or remove unwanted material. *The school computers contain special software to filter viruses.*

gen•der
(**jen**-dur)

noun the sex of a person or animal; male or female. *How you decide to dress or wear your hair often depends on your gender.*

ha•bit
(**ha**-bit)

noun something a person does regularly, usually without thinking. *Biting your nails is a bad habit.*

har•ass
(huh-**rass**)

verb to frequently annoy or bother someone and make his or her life unpleasant. *I don't like it when people harass others by calling them names.*

har•ass•ment
(huh-**rass**-mehnt)

noun the act of frequently annoying or bothering someone. *In our school, you can be suspended for harassment against another student.*

ACADEMIC GLOSSARY

i•deal
(eye-**deel**)
adjective   the best that something or someone can be. *My ideal vacation would be a trip to Africa.*

i•den•ti•ty
(eye-**den**-ti-tee)
noun   a sense of self; a feeling of belonging to a particular group or race. *My cheerful attitude is a huge part of my personal identity.*

im•age
(**im**-ij)
noun   a photograph or picture, which might be real or imagined. *The newspaper printed an image of the criminal.*

im•pact
(**im**-pakt)
1. *noun*   the effect of one thing on another. *The student council's decisions have an impact on everyone at school.*

2. *verb*   to have an effect on someone or something. *Pollution from cars can impact the environment in many serious ways.*

im•ple•ment
(**im**-pluh-muhnt)
verb   to begin a plan or process. *Our principal wants to implement an after-school language program.*

im•ple•men•ta•tion
(im-pluh-mehn-**tay**-shuhn)
noun   the act of making a plan or process happen. *So far, the implementation of the new anti-bullying rule has been a success.*

in•come
(**in**-kuhm)
noun   money that a person regularly earns from a job or other source. *A part-time job is often a good source of income.*

in•crease
(in-**kreess**)
verb   to make or become larger. *To get better grades, you need to increase the amount of time you spend studying.*

in•di•vid•u•al
(in-duh-**vij**-oo-uhl)
noun   one person, considered separately from a larger group. *Our teacher asked one individual to speak for everyone in the class.*

in•e•qual•i•ty
(in-i-**kwol**-uh-tee)
noun   an unfair situation in which some groups have less than others. *Years ago, there was much more inequality between men and women than there is today.*

in•flu•ence
(**in**-floo-uhnss)

1. *noun*   the power that someone or something has to affect others. *Music videos sometimes have an influence over the songs teens buy for their MP3 players.*

2. *verb*   to affect what someone does, says, or believes. *The weather can influence how people dress.*

in•ter•ac•tive
(in-tur-**ak**-tiv)

adjective   referring to technology that can send and respond to commands or messages. *The video games' many interactive features make them interesting to play.*

in•ter•pret
(in-**tur**-prit)

verb   to determine the meaning of something. *For homework, we had to interpret the meaning of our favorite poem.*

in•volved
(in-**volvd**)

adjective   connected with an activity or event in some way. *I work on stage crew because I enjoy being involved with the school play.*

is•sue
(**ish**-yoo)

noun   a topic or problem. *The school board debated the issue of whether or not junk food should be sold in the cafeteria.*

le•gal
(**lee**-guhl)

adjective   allowed by law. *In our state, it is legal to drive a car if you are over the age of 16.*

leg•is•la•tion
(lej-uh-**slay**-shuhn)

noun   a law or group of laws. *The new town legislation does not allow loud music in the park after 8:00 P.M.*

lit•ter
(**lit**-tur)

verb   to leave trash lying around. *We picked up all the garbage from our picnic because it is illegal to litter in the park.*

man•da•to•ry
(**man**-duh-tor-ee)

adjective   describing something that must be done. *Going to school every day is mandatory for kids under the age of 16.*

me•di•a
(**mee**-dee-uh)

noun   organizations that provide news and information to the public, such as TV shows and magazines. *My brother got a job in media because he is very interested in current events.*

meth•od
(**meth**-uhd)

noun   a specific way of doing something. *The substitute teacher taught us a new method of solving the math problem.*

ACADEMIC GLOSSARY

min•i•mum
(**min**-uh-muhm)
adjective   describing the smallest amount allowed or needed. *Ali turned in the minimum number of pages needed for the research paper assignment.*

mon•i•tor
(**mon**-uh-tur)
verb   to carefully watch and check a person or situation. *You should closely monitor a pot of water boiling on the stove.*

mo•rale
(muh-**ral**)
noun   the level of positive feelings and confidence that people have. *Our school's morale improved greatly once the football team won its first game.*

mo•ti•vate
(**moh**-tuh-vate)
verb   to make someone want to work hard to achieve something. *Mr. Hanzel likes to motivate his students by ordering pizza when the class does well on a test.*

mo•ti•va•ted
(**moh**-tuh-vay-tid)
adjective   wanting to work hard to achieve something. *The coach gave the team a last-minute pep talk so that they were motivated when they took the field.*

neg•a•tive
(**neg**-uh-tiv)
adjective   bad or harmful; not showing any sign of what a medical or scientific test is looking for. *Exhaust from cars can have a negative effect on the environment.*

nu•tri•tion
(noo-**trih**-shuhn)
noun   the process of eating foods that are good for a person's health. *Sam takes a vitamin every day to boost his nutrition.*

nu•tri•tious
(noo-**trish**-uhss)
adjective   good for a person's health. *I am trying to eat less sugar because I know it is not very nutritious.*

o•bese
(oh-**beess**)
adjective   so overweight that it is dangerous. *After years of overeating, my aunt is now obese and experiencing health problems.*

o•be•si•ty
(oh-**beess**-ih-tee)
noun   the condition of being so overweight that it is dangerous. *Too much fast food can lead to obesity.*

ob•sess
(uhb-**sess**)
verb   to think about or have an unhealthy interest in something or someone. *I think it's dangerous that you obsess about building muscles.*

ob•ses•sion
(uhb-**sesh**-uhn)

noun   an unhealthy interest in something or someone. *Cara has developed an obsession with makeup and dieting.*

ob•tain
(uhb-**tayn**)

verb   to get something using effort. *The soccer team sold magazine subscriptions to obtain money for new uniforms.*

oc•cur
(uh-**kur**)

verb   to take place or happen. *Fire drills occur twice a month at our school.*

op•po•nent
(uh-**poh**-nuhnt)

noun   someone you try to beat; someone who disagrees with a plan or idea. *Surprisingly, the lowest-ranked team turned out to be our toughest opponent.*

op•tion
(**op**-shuhn)

noun   a choice. *I looked at every option before I decided to have salad for lunch.*

per•ceive
(pur-**seev**)

verb   to see or think of someone or something in a certain way. *Sometimes people perceive me as shy because I don't talk very much.*

per•cent
(pur-**sent**)

noun   a part of a whole measured by one in one hundred. *I got ninety percent of the questions right on the last vocabulary test.*

per•cep•tion
(pur-**sep**-shuhn)

noun   the way something is thought about and the idea of what it is like. *My perception of my teacher is that he is a nice, helpful person.*

pol•i•cy
(**pol**-uh-see)

noun   a rule. *Our town has a very strict policy against graffiti.*

po•lit•i•cal
(puh-**lit**-i-kuhl)

adjective   relating to government. *The presidential candidates debated the political issues they most cared about.*

pol•lute
(puh-**loot**)

verb   to release or cause harmful materials that damage or contaminate the air, water, or soil. *The oil spill taught me about the damage that occurs when people pollute the ocean.*

pol•lu•tion
(puh-**loo**-shuhn)

noun   harmful materials that damage or contaminate the air, water, and soil. *Exhaust from cars can cause air pollution.*

ACADEMIC GLOSSARY

po•ten•tial
(puh-**ten**-shuhl)
adjective   likely to develop into something in the future. *My neighbor is a potential customer of my dog-walking business since she has three dogs.*

pre•vent
(pri-**vent**)
verb   to stop something from happening. *Brushing your teeth can help prevent cavities.*

pre•ven•tion
(pri-**vent**-shuhn)
noun   the act of stopping something from happening. *During fire prevention week, we learned how to put out different kinds of fires.*

pri•mar•y
(**prye**-mair-ee)
adjective   main or most important. *Getting a lead role in the school play was Jorge's primary goal.*

pri•va•cy
(**prye**-vuh-see)
noun   the state of being able to avoid public attention. *Many celebrities do not have enough privacy since people are always trying to photograph them.*

pri•vate
(**prye**-vit)
adjective   avoiding the attention of others. *Josie had a private conversation with the teacher after all the students left.*

prog•ress
(**prog**-ruhss)
noun   a slow change for the better. *After we watered the plants for several weeks, we saw progress in their growth.*

pro•hib•it
(proh-**hib**-it)
verb   to forbid or not allow an action. *Many public places prohibit smoking indoors.*

pro•mote
(pruh-**mote**)
verb   to help something become more successful or well-known. *The school had a health fair to promote good nutrition and exercise.*

pro•tect
(pruh-**tekt**)
verb   to keep safe from harm or attack. *When I ride my bike, I always wear a helmet to protect my head.*

pro•tec•tion
(pruh-**tek**-shuhn)
noun   the state of being kept safe from harm or attack. *The alarm system in my house provides protection against robbery.*

ran•dom
(**ran**-duhm)
adjective   done or chosen without a specific plan or pattern. *To be fair, the gym teacher chose the teams at random.*

rate
(**rayt**)

noun   the number of times that something happens during a period of time. *During a run, the rate at which my heart beats increases.*

re•ac•tion
(ree-**ak**-shuhn)

noun   something that a person feels or does in response to something. *When our teacher told us there would be no test today, my first reaction was to ask why.*

re•al•is•tic
(ree-uh-**liss**-tik)

adjective   possible or practical. *I know it's not the most realistic goal, but I still want to be a professional basketball player.*

reb•el
(**reb**-uhl)

noun   someone who fights against ideas or people that he or she disagrees with. *Tawana wanted to be a rebel, so she dyed her hair purple and pink.*

re•cy•cle
(ree-**sye**-kuhl)

verb   to put used objects through a process so they can be made into something new. *Our school has special containers so that we can recycle bottles, cans, and paper.*

re•duce
(ri-**dooss**)

verb   to make something smaller or less than it was before. *If I wake up earlier, I will reduce my chance of being late again.*

re•duced
(ri-**doost**)

adjective   smaller or less than it was before. *I decided to buy the book because the price was reduced.*

reg•u•la•tion
(reg-yuh-**lay**-shuhn)

noun   an official rule or order. *If we don't follow every regulation during the game, we may be disqualified.*

rel•e•vant
(**rel**-uh-vuhnt)

adjective   directly relating to an issue or matter. *Steven checked out all the books that were relevant to his report on whales and dolphins.*

re•ly
(ri-**lye**)

verb   to depend on someone or something. *I rely on my friends to cheer me up when I'm in a bad mood.*

re•mov•al
(ri-**moov**-uhl)

noun   the act of taking something away. *At home, the removal of trash is one of my daily chores.*

re•move
(ri-**moov**)

verb to take something away. *The referee warned that she would remove the player from the game if he continued to be rude.*

re•place
(ri-**playss**)

verb to put something or someone in place of another. *Should I replace this video game with the new version that's coming out?*

re•place•ment
(ri-**playss**-mehnt)

noun something or someone that has been put in place of another. *I had to get a replacement for the cell phone I lost.*

rep•re•sent
(rep-ri-**zent**)

verb to be a sign or mark that means something. *Maps use symbols to represent roads, oceans, parks, and hotels.*

re•quire
(ri-**kwire**)

verb to demand something by law or rule. *Some part-time jobs require that you work only 20 hours per week.*

re•quire•ment
(ri-**kwire**-muhnt)

noun something that must be done by law or rule. *One requirement of the project was that we include a piece of art.*

re•search
(**ree**-surch)

1. *noun* careful study and investigation to discover new facts or test ideas. *I did lots of research before starting my paper on roller coasters.*

2. *verb* to study a subject in detail. *It's always more fun to research topics that interest you.*

re•source
(**ree**-sorss)

noun available land, water, and natural energy that can be used; something used to make life easier. *The sun is a natural resource people haven't learned to use fully.*

re•sponse
(ri-**sponss**)

noun something that is said, written, or done as a reaction or reply to something or someone. *What was your response to Kendra's party invitation?*

re•spon•si•bil•i•ty
(ri-spon-suh-**bil**-uh-tee)

noun the duty to be in charge of or look after something or someone. *While our teacher was out sick, the responsibility for our class went to a substitute.*

re•spon•si•ble
(ri-**spon**-suh-buhl)

adjective having a duty to be in charge of or look after something or someone. *When my parents go out, I am responsible for taking care of my younger sister.*

re•strict
(ri-**strikt**)

verb to limit the size, amount, or range of something. *My mom restricts the amount of time I spend on the Internet.*

re•tail
(**ree**-tayl)

adjective having to do with selling products. *I like to spend my allowance at my favorite retail stores.*

re•tail•ers
(**ree**-tay-lurs)

noun people or businesses that sell products to customers. *Some retailers offer free gifts if you spend a certain amount of money.*

re•u•sa•ble
(ree-**yoo**-zuh-buhl)

adjective capable of being used more than once. *Reusable bags help protect the environment because they don't create more trash.*

re•use
(ree-**yooz**)

verb to utilize something more than once. *I reuse old cereal boxes by using them to store magazines.*

re•veal
(ri-**veel**)

verb to make known something that was unknown or secret; to show. *At the end of the show, the magician revealed how to perform some of the tricks.*

se•cu•ri•ty
(si-**kyoo**-ruh-tee)

noun the state of being free from risk or danger. *Airports have metal detectors to help improve security.*

se•lect
(si-**lekt**)

verb to pick out or choose. *I select a clean shirt to wear every morning.*

shift
(**shift**)

verb to change attention, direction, or focus from one thing to another. *The teacher asked us to shift our attention from our textbooks to the math problem on the board.*

sig•nif•i•cant
(sig-**nif**-uh-kuhnt)

adjective large or important enough to have an effect on something. *The cast spent a significant amount of time rehearsing for the school play.*

sim•i•lar
(**sim**-uh-lur)

adjective almost the same. *People often ask if Khalil and I are brothers because we have such similar features.*

so•cial
(**soh**-shuhl)

adjective relating to the way people spend time with others. *I enjoy going to parties, concerts, and other social events.*

ACADEMIC GLOSSARY

strat•e•gy
(**strat**-uh-jee)
noun   a plan for making something
happen. *The coach had an excellent
strategy for how to beat the other team.*

suf•fi•cient
(suh-**fish**-uhnt)
adjective   enough for a specific purpose.
*Ms. Fraser said that one page would be
sufficient for the essay.*

sus•pend
(suhs-**pend**)
verb   to officially stop something
temporarily. *My mom made sure to
suspend the newspaper delivery before we
went on vacation.*

tar•get
(**tar**-git)
1. *noun*   someone or something that is
chosen for attack. *If you aim for the target
on the backboard, you'll be more likely to
make the shot.*

2. *verb*   to direct attention toward a
specific person, group, or item. *Extra
sit-ups will definitely target your stomach
muscles.*

tax
(**taks**)
noun   money paid to the government for
public services, such as education and
roads. *The additional tax on clothing will
help raise money for new textbooks.*

tech•nol•o•gy
(tek-**nol**-uh-jee)
noun   the use of science and computers
to do everyday tasks. *I don't know how
my parents grew up without the technology
we have today.*

threat
(**thret**)
noun   a statement that expresses
something bad will happen. *When the
cyberbully made a threat against Mia, she
reported it immediately to the principal.*

threat•en
(**thret**-uhn)
verb   to make a statement that expresses
the possibility that something bad will
happen. *My parents know that if they
threaten to take away my game system, I'll
usually do what they tell me.*

tox•ic
(**tok**-sik)
adjective   containing poison. *It is
important to store toxic material where
young children and pets can't reach it.*

tru•an•cy
(**troo**-uhn-see)
noun   the act of purposely staying away
from school without permission. *In many
places, truancy is against the law because it
is dangerous for students.*

tru•ant

(**troo**-uhnt)

noun   a student who stays away from school without permission. *Being a truant will get you into serious trouble with your parents and teachers.*

tu•tor•ing

(**too**-tur-ing)

noun   the act of privately teaching someone. *Alison had trouble with reading, so her teacher suggested after-school tutoring.*

un•re•al•is•tic

(uhn-ree-uh-**liss**-tik)

adjective   not possible or practical. *The way that movie portrayed space travel was completely unrealistic.*

van•dal

(**van**-duhl)

noun   someone who purposely damages things, especially public property. *Have the police caught the vandals who broke the swings in the park?*

van•dal•ism

(**van**-duhl-izm)

noun   the act of purposely damaging things, especially public property. *You will be automatically suspended if you commit any vandalism at school.*

vic•tim

(**vik**-tuhm)

noun   a person who has been injured or harmed by someone else. *Peter was the victim of a car accident, but he wasn't seriously injured.*

vi•o•late

(**vye**-uh-late)

verb   to do something that makes someone feel attacked. *I don't like it when people violate my privacy by going through my backpack.*

vi•o•lence

(**vye**-uh-luhnss)

noun   the use of great force or strength to hurt or destroy. *With so many crime shows, I see more violence on TV than I do in real life.*

vi•o•lent

(**vye**-uh-luhnt)

adjective   involving actions that are likely to hurt or kill people. *The meteorologist warned that a violent storm would hit our town this evening.*

CREDITS